TABLE

*The LORD spoke to Moses in the Tent of Meeting in the
Desert of Sinai (1:1).*

—— 1 ——

Moses and Aaron
Number the People
Numbers 1–4

The Book of Numbers provides an essential link in Israel's story. It tells of the departure from Sinai, scene of God's revelation of covenant and law; forty years of wandering in the desert; and the arrival at the threshold of the Promised Land. Furthermore, the book recounts events and legal regulations connected with census, tabernacle, Levites and priests, encampment, and desert testing.

The book's name is somewhat misleading, since it refers to the census activity, which is found only in Chapters 1–4 and again in Chapter 26. The Hebrew title, "In the desert," is based on a phrase in 1:1 and more accurately describes the experience portrayed in these thirty-six chapters.

DIMENSION ONE:
WHAT DOES THE BIBLE SAY?

Answer these questions by reading Numbers 1

1. Where are the children of Israel when Numbers begins? (1:1)

2. Where does God speak to Moses? (1:1)

3. What does the Lord tell Moses to do? Why? (1:1-3)

4. Moses numbers twelve groups. What are the names and the count given for each group? (1:20-46)

Group		Name	Number
One	(1:20-21)		
Two	(1:22-23)		
Three	(1:24-25)		
Four	(1:26-27)		
Five	(1:28-29)		
Six	(1:30-31)		
Seven	(1:32-33)		
Eight	(1:34-35)		
Nine	(1:36-37)		
Ten	(1:38-39)		
Eleven	(1:40-41)		
Twelve	(1:42-43)		

5. Which important tribe is omitted? Why? (1:47-53)

Answer these questions by reading Numbers 2

6. Where are the Israelites to camp? (2:2)

7. The twelve tribes are divided into four groups of three tribes each. Which tribes are located in each of the directions below?

East (2:3-9)

South (2:10-16)

West (2:18-24)

North (2:25-31)

8. The Tent of Meeting is in the middle of the camp. Who encamps closest to it? (2:17)

Answer these questions by reading Numbers 3

9. What is the work of the Levites? (3:5-8)

10. For whom are the Levites a substitute? (3:11-13)

11. How does the numbering of the Levites differ from the general census described in 1:3? (3:15)

12. The three Levite groups are assigned places around the Tabernacle and responsibilities for its maintenance. What are the location and work of each group?

Name	Location	Responsibility

Gershonites
(3:21-26)

Kohathites
(3:27-31)

Merarites
(3:33-37)

13. Who camps east of the Tabernacle? (3:38)

Answer these questions by reading Numbers 4

14. Who is Moses to count in the third census? (4:2-3, 22-23, 29-30)

15. What is the special work of the sons of Aaron? (4:5-14)

16. What does the Lord specify about holy things? (4:15, 18-20)

17. Each group of the Levites is to carry certain things when the Israelites travel. Are these the same as those indicated in Chapter 3? (4:4, 25-26, 31-32)

DIMENSION TWO:
WHAT DOES THE BIBLE MEAN?

The study of the text of Numbers 1–4 shows us that these chapters are full of names and figures, most of them new and strange to us. It is important to learn this information if we are to know what the text says. It is more important, however, to go beyond data-gathering in our search for understanding. We need to remember that the biblical story is written to express a living faith in God, who works in human history. We can understand Numbers 1–4 more fully if we look for the faith to which Israel witnesses through the details and events of the story found in Numbers.

❑ *Numbers 1:1.* The setting for the initial action of Numbers is the same as that of Exodus 19–Leviticus 27. The Israelites are still at Sinai, the scene of God's revelation of law and covenant. The location of Sinai remains a mystery. Some persons agree with the tradition that places it in the extreme southern section of the Sinai Peninsula while others have suggested a site farther north near Kadesh.

The biblical writer places the census at one month after the establishment of the Tabernacle (Exodus 40:17), an event dated at exactly one year after the Exodus from Egypt. The writer of Exodus 24–40, Leviticus 1–27, and much of Numbers is concerned with exact times and dates.

The Lord commands Moses to take a census. This word comes to him in the "Tent of Meeting." The writer of Leviticus and this section of Numbers uses this phrase to denote the Tabernacle, which, as we discovered in Dimension One, stood in the center of the Israelite camp. The Tent is the concrete expression of Israel's early faith that God's presence was with them as they moved about.

❑ *Numbers 1:20-46.* The groups listed in the census are the twelve tribes of Israel. Several such lists exists in the first five books of the Bible, and it is interesting to compare them. (See, for example, Genesis 29:31–30:24; Genesis 49; and Deuteronomy 33.) The lists always include twelve tribes but not all the names are identical from list to list.

The number of men able to go to war totals 603,550. The greatness of this number (which makes the Israelites altogether total over two million) has puzzled biblical scholars. One scholar suggests that the word for thousand (*'eleph*) has been misunderstood and should be read as "subgroup." Another suggests that the numbers from David's later census (2 Samuel 24:1-4) have been inserted here.

❑ *Numbers 1:47-53.* The Levites are set aside as a special group with responsibility for the Tabernacle. They are to encamp around it, have charge of its care, and provide for its movement when the people move. The Tabernacle is holy, and only those appointed to its service can have contact with it. All others are punished by death if they touch it.

❑ *Numbers 2:1-34.* These groupings reflect the traditional genealogy of Genesis 29–30. Judah, Leah's fourth son and ancestor of the dominant Israelite tribe, is placed in the honored position—east of the Tabernacle. Attached to this group are Issachar and Zebulun, Leah's fifth and sixth sons. This eastern group is first in the marching order when Israel strikes camp.

In second position (encamped on the south), is the tribe of Reuben, first-born of Jacob and Leah, accompanied by Simeon, Leah's second son. Levi, the third son, is not listed here because his tribe has been set aside for special service. He is replaced by Gad, the older of two sons born to Zilpah, Leah's maid.

The group on the west, third in the order of march, is composed of Rachel's descendants. Ephraim and Manasseh, Joseph's sons, and Benjamin form this group.

The northern group is made up of Dan, son of Rachel's handmaid, Bilhah; Naphtali, second son of Bilhah; and Asher, second son of Zilpah. These so-called concubine tribes—sons of Jacob by the handmaids of Leah and Rachel—make up the fourth group.

❑ *Numbers 3:1- 4.* The "sons of Aaron" designates the priestly group that has authority over the levitical family. Throughout Israel's history, the specially ordained Aaronites are regarded as important priests, for they serve directly at the altar and offer sacrifices. Although the genealogies credit Aaron with four sons, this passage explains why only two function in later times as priestly families. Leviticus 10:1-3 recounts the story of Nadab and Abihu.

❑ *Numbers 3:5-10.* The relationship of the Levites and Aaronite priests receives frequent attention in the Old Testament. Here the Lord gives the Levites important duties, but the Levites are subservient to Aaron and his sons. Only the Aaronites are empowered for full priesthood.

❑ *Numbers 3:14-16.* Moses is to number all Levites over a month old. The lower age stipulation is due to the fact that the first-born are consecrated at one month. Since the Levite census is connected with their role as substitutes for Israel's first-born, the corresponding age is used.

❑ *Numbers 4:1-33.* The second numbering of the Levites is a "head count" for service and includes those from ages thirty to fifty. These verses specify the role of each levitical group when Israel marches. The areas of responsibility are much like those in Chapter 3. The sons of Aaron still occupy a special place. The dynamic and fearsome power of holiness makes their service indispensable and unique. (See especially verses 15, 18-20.)

DIMENSION THREE:
WHAT DOES THE BIBLE MEAN TO ME?

Numbers 1:2-4, 17-19—The Israelite Census

The major activity of the first four chapters of Numbers is the counting of certain groups of people. In Numbers, the census is taken in obedience to God's command, but an entirely different picture is presented in David's later census (2 Samuel 24 or 1 Chronicles 12). God judges the later census as sinful and punishes Israel severely.

What are the differences between the two numberings? Why is one considered motivated by God and the other by Satan? What do the two numberings imply about governmental information-gathering and the responsibilities of government leaders in the use of the data?

Numbers 1:20-46—Family Ties

The tribal list is a prominent feature in Israel's recital of history. It occurs at such significant points as the death of Jacob (Genesis 49), the death of Moses (Deuteronomy 34), and the Conquest of Canaan (Joshua 13–19; Judges 1). While the list varies somewhat from place to place, it is remarkably uniform. The number of tribes is always twelve, the central group remains essentially the same, and the groupings are constant—reflecting a tradition of historical and geographical relationships. What meaning do you see in this recounting with regard to personal identification and family history?

The prominence of tribal identification in the story of Israel indicates that they always regard themselves as members of a distinct family, related to other families. These families make up Israel, God's people. No person's existence can be fully understood apart from membership in a family. In what ways is membership in your family important to you?

What does this tradition of ancestry and relationship suggest about our life in the church today? What does it teach us about using tradition as a resource for living now?

Numbers 2—Pilgrimage

The concern for matters of encampment and march provides a helpful model for the life of God's people in all periods of history. The Israelites recounted the stories of their wandering and encampment long after settling in Canaan. These stories evidently were important to them in their settled life. The church also has found significance in Israel's wilderness journey. While the detail of this chapter is somewhat tiresome, the stance of readiness and preparation for setting out on the march indicates an important aspect of the life of the people of God. How does this picture of people on pilgrimage fit our idea of the church today? What factors in our church life interfere with the concept of pilgrimage? What new meaning does this image give to our understanding of the church and our faithfulness in Christian living?

Numbers 1:47; 2:17; 3:1-51; 4:11-33—Clergy and Laity

One of the major themes of Numbers 1–4 is the commitment of worship responsibility to the Levites. However, only the "sons of Aaron" are allowed to officiate at the altar and handle the most sacred objects. But together the Levites and Aaronites are a special group commissioned by God to provide for and carry out the worship of Israel. If Israel is itself a holy nation—chosen to serve God in a particular way—why is there a need for Levites and Aaronites?

These passages help us address issues about the church and its ministry. The relation of clergy and laity, the nature of lay ministry, and the role of ordained clergy are all matters for serious consideration in our day. What elements in these passages help us define the role of ordained ministry today?

*The LORD turn his face toward you and give you peace
(6:26).*

2

Laws and Regulations

Numbers 5–9

**DIMENSION ONE:
WHAT DOES THE BIBLE SAY?**

Answer these questions by reading Numbers 5

1. Who are the people of Israel to remove from camp? Why?
   (5:1-3)

2. How does one make restitution for wrongs done to others?
   (5:5-8)

3. What does a husband do if he suspects his wife of unfaithfulness? (5:11-15)

4. What does the priest make the suspected wife do?
   (5:18-22, 26)

5. How is the guilt or innocence of the wife known? (5:27-28)

Answer these questions by reading Numbers 6

6. What are the three conditions of the Nazarite vow? (6:1-8)

7. What offerings is a Nazarite to bring when he completes his vow? (6:13-15)

8. What does the Nazarite do with his hair? (6:18)

9. What does the wave offering include? (6:19-20)

10. With what words are Aaron and his sons to bless Israel? (6:22-26)

Answer these questions by reading Numbers 7

11. What offerings do the tribal leaders bring to the Tabernacle? What is their use? (7:1-5)

12. What gifts does Nahshon of the tribe of Judah bring on the first day? (7:12-17)

13. The other eleven tribal representatives bring identical gifts on successive days. In what order do the tribes come? (7:18-83)

14. When Moses speaks with the Lord, where is the voice of the Lord located? (7:89)

Answer these questions by reading Numbers 8

15. How is Aaron to set up the seven lamps? (8:1-3)

16. What are the Levites to do in the ritual of cleansing? (8:5-9)

17. What kind of offering are the Levites themselves? (8:10-11)

18. Why are the Levites the Lord's own? (8:14-18)

19. What are the years of service for a Levite? (8:23-26)

Answer these questions by reading Numbers 9

20. When is Israel to observe the Passover? (9:2-3)

21. How are those absent or "unclean" at that time to observe the festival? (9:6-12)

22. What is the provision for aliens among them? (9:14)

23. How do the children of Israel know when to make camp and when to set out? (9:15-17)

DIMENSION TWO:
WHAT DOES THE BIBLE MEAN?

❏ *Numbers 5:1-4.* While still at Sinai, Israel receives more instructions. These instructions seem somewhat miscellaneous, but verse 3 states the theme that holds them together. Since the Lord dwells with them in their camp, they must see that it is kept pure and undefiled.

❏ *Numbers 5:5-10.* Verse 6 is somewhat unclear as to the kinds of sins it addresses. The Hebrew says "the sins of man." Older translations such as the Revised Standard Version leave it ambiguous by translating it "sins that men commit." The NIV, however, renders it "when a man or woman wrongs another in any way." This translation is probably closer to the original meaning. The provision for restitution in the following verse makes it clear that sin in verse 6 refers to wrongs committed against another human being. Such misconduct is regarded as breaking faith with the Lord.

❏ *Numbers 6:1-21.* The Nazirites are mentioned in several places in the Old Testament, but these verses are the only ones that specify their vows. Becoming a Nazarite involves abstaining from wine, refraining from cutting the hair, and avoiding contact with a dead body.

Verses 1-21 make it clear that this Nazarite vow is temporary. The completion rite involves a range of offerings, indicating the seriousness with which the vow is taken. The hair is shaved off and burned with the peace offering to prevent defilement of the hair grown during the period of the vow.

❏ *Numbers 6:22-27.* Aaron's blessing contains several words that are significant. "Bless" relates to well-being and prosperity. "Keep" means to care for and protect from evil. "Turn his face toward you" signifies divine favor. The first clause in verse 25 can be translated "bestow favor upon you." The word *peace* in the Old Testament means wholeness.

❏ *Numbers 7:1-9.* Exodus 40:17 identifies the day when the Tabernacle was set up as the first day of the first month of the second year after the Exodus from Egypt. Numbers 1:1 dates the census of Chapters 1–4 as beginning on the first day of the second month of the second year. Therefore, the account in Chapter 7 is a kind of flashback, since these events preceded those of the previous chapters by a month.

❏ *Numbers 7:10-88.* In addition to the covered carts and oxen of verses 1-9, the leaders bring dedicatory offerings for the altar. The lavishness of the offering raises a question about the possibility of such wealth among a group of fleeing slaves in the wilderness. Perhaps the writer wants to encourage later readers to provide a full range of sacrificial offerings, even though times may be difficult.

❑ *Numbers 7:89.* In Exodus 25:22, when God instructs Moses to build the ark, God tells Moses that he will speak to him from above the ark and from between the cherubim when the ark is completed. This verse describes the fulfillment of that promise.

❑ *Numbers 8:5-22.* This section considers the rituals by which Levites come into their life of service. Verses 5-13 specify certain cleansing rites. The "water of cleansing" is intended to free them from sin. The shaving of the whole body and the washing of clothes have the purpose of cleansing from impurity. The people's laying their hands on the Levites emphasizes the fact that the Levites offer their service on behalf of all Israel.

❑ *Numbers 9:1-14.* These verses tell of the second Passover. The Israelites are to observe this festival in memory of their deliverance, which they identify with the first Passover. If one misses the Passover because of uncleanness or unavoidable absence, that person is to observe the festival exactly one month later, on the fourteenth day of the second month. Observance of the festival is more important than exact schedule.

DIMENSION THREE:
WHAT DOES THE BIBLE MEAN TO ME?

Numbers 5:1-31—Responsibility in Relationship

Part of this chapter (verses 5-10) addresses conduct that endangers the common life of God's people. The effect of wrong against individuals is recognized as harmful to God and to the whole people of God. It is more than a simple matter between two people. It breaks faith with God and endangers community life.

Where are people in our society being deprived of what is rightfully theirs? If sins against persons are sins against God, what is the church to do in such cases of deprivation?

Verses 11-31 address the point of distrust in marriage relationships, but in a prejudiced way. The woman must prove her innocence. No provision is made to deal with the possibility of a husband's unfaithfulness. Later writings handle this concern more equitably.

However, the basic premise of the regulation—that breach of family relationship is a serious wrong—is important. How do Christians deal with this concern today?

Numbers 6:1-21—Special Commitment

In the law, Israel provides for the taking of special vows. The persons who do so are called Nazirites. These vows witnessed to a strong commitment in the midst of everyday living. Does some vow of commitment have value in our religious life today?

We are not part of God's people by virtue of birth (as in Israel). We become members by taking the vows of church membership. As you consider your own church membership vows, do you see any comparison between them and the Nazarite vows? Do they express commitment in similar ways? What does this passage in Numbers say to us about the way we commit ourselves and carry out our vows?

Numbers 6:22-27—The Blessing of God

The familiarity of this passage indicates its continued use in worship from earliest times to the present. Traditionally used at the close of public worship, the intent of the blessing is to bestow on the worshiper the continued blessing of God.

The blessing theme in the Old Testament points to the ever-present Creator God who makes all things good and stands ready to bestow divine gifts on humanity. While we use this blessing regularly in our worship, we seldom consider what it says about the nature of God. What meaning does this blessing have for you?

Numbers 7–9—Preparation for Pilgrimage

As the people prepare to leave Sinai, attention turns from general regulations to specific measures that will ready the

LAWS AND REGULATIONS **17**

people for the journey. These measures are not the concerns for provisions and transportation that we might expect. They are those things that will enable Israel to maintain a clear sense of identity as the people of God in their journey.

The first element in this preparation is the completion and consecration of the Tabernacle. As Israel looks back on their days in the desert, this mobile worship center provided the focus for Israel's life while on march. Behind all the details of the story in Chapter 7 lies the assumption that the uniting fact of Israel's existence is the expression of faith through worship. What are the values of the church's worship as you experience them? How does worship help to unify the church?

The second element in Israel's preparation for her desert journey is the consecration of the Levites (Numbers 8). The Levites are Israel's offering to the Lord. Does this image help us understand the clergy's role in our church? How can the clergy be regarded as the offering of the church to God? How does this understanding fit with the concept of clergy as called of God?

The third element in Israel's preparation (Numbers 9:1-14) is the celebration of the Passover. Festival observance is an important part of our church year. Why do we celebrate festivals? What function do they serve? How do they help us become more aware of ourselves as the church?

Finally, the story comes to the theme of God's guidance in Israel's desert experience (Numbers 9:15-23). The cloud indicates when Israel is to move and when Israel is to remain. How does the theme of divine guidance in pilgrimage find expression in the church today? How does it apply to us individually? How can we differentiate between the time for waiting and the time for marching?

The LORD said to Moses, "Send some men to explore the land of Canaan" (13:1-2).

—— 3 ——
The Long Journey Begins
Numbers 10–14

DIMENSION ONE:
WHAT DOES THE BIBLE SAY?

Answer these questions by reading Numbers 10

1. What does God tell Moses to make? For what are these to be used? (10:1-10)

2. How do the people know they are to move from Sinai? (10:11-12)

3. When the Israelites set out from Sinai, where do the Levites march? What is their task? (10:14-21)

4. What goes before the children of Israel when they leave Sinai? (10:33)

5. How does the Lord respond to the people's complaining? (11:1)

6. What do the Israelites crave? Why? (11:4-6)

7. Why is Moses troubled? (11:10-15)

8. What does the Lord promise Israel? (11:18-23)

9. When the seventy elders go with Moses to the Tent of Meeting, what happens to them? (11:24-25)

10. What meat does God provide for Israel? What happens as they eat? (11:31-33)

Answer these questions by reading Numbers 12

11. Who raises questions about Moses' leadership and why? (12:1-2)

12. What makes Moses different from other prophets? (12:6-8)

13. What happens to Miriam? (12:9-10, 13-15)

Answer these questions by reading Numbers 13

14. Where does God tell Moses to send the twelve representatives of the tribes of Israel? (13:1-15)

15. What are the explorers to find out? (13:17-20)

16. What is the explorers' report when they return? (13:27-28)

17. What is Caleb's advice? (13:30)

18. What do the other explorers say? (13:31-33)

Answer these questions by reading Numbers 14

19. How do the people of Israel react to this report? (14:1-4)

20. What happens when Caleb and Joshua urge the Israelites to go into Canaan? (14:6-10)

21. When God threatens to destroy Israel, what does Moses do? (14:13-19)

22. What punishment does God place upon Israel? (14:20-35)

23. Who are the exceptions? (14:30, 38)

DIMENSION TWO:
WHAT DOES THE BIBLE MEAN?

❏ *Numbers 10:11-28.* By referring to Exodus 19:1, we can deduce that the Israelites left Sinai eleven months and nineteen days after their arrival there. The departure time is nineteen days after the start of the census (Numbers 1:1). They follow the order of march already provided in Chapter 2.

The location of the Desert of Paran, the place toward which Israel journeys, is uncertain. It appears, however, to have been in the north central part of the Sinai peninsula, an area south of the land of Canaan.

❏ *Numbers 11:1-3.* These verses explain the origin of the place name *Taberah.* Taberah comes from the root word that means "to burn." The story emphasizes the theme of Israel's complaining and is one of several where this theme is mentioned in the desert account.

The Lord's anger is kindled by the people's complaints, but is stayed from consuming Israel by Moses' intercession. This kind of intervention is a recurring theme of the desert narrative and tells us about the place and role Moses had in Israel's traditions.

❑ *Numbers 11:4-34.* This passage emphasizes the complaining theme that runs through the desert account. God's people, who had cried out for freedom and deliverance when enslaved in Egypt, now raise bitter cries against God whenever problems arise. They remember the food of Egypt with fondness but forget their cries for God's intervention against their slavemasters.

❑ *Numbers 12:1-16.* The identity of Moses' wife here is a puzzle. In Exodus, Moses' wife is Zipporah, the daughter of the Midianite priest. If Cushite refers to an Ethiopian, then Moses has taken a second wife. However, Habakkuk 3:7 refers to Cushan and Midian. On this basis, Cushite might be understood as Midianite, and the reference could be to Zipporah.

We are not told what Miriam and Aaron find to criticize in Moses' wife. It is clear, however, that they set themselves against Moses and his leadership. This is the first of a number of rebellions against Moses.

One of the main traditions about Moses in the Old Testament is his standing as a prophet, a spokesman for God. Here Aaron and Miriam claim that they, too, are prophets. Indeed, Miriam is elsewhere called a prophetess (Exodus 15:20).

In Chapter 11, the topic is the sharing of the prophetic function with seventy elders. But here, the emphasis is on Moses' superiority over other prophets. Prophets receive oracles and speak for God to the people. They receive their information through visions and dreams, but Moses speaks directly with God.

Notice the characteristics of Moses in this story. He is meek, that is, modest and dependent upon God. He is a superior prophet, receiving his word firsthand. He intercedes for Miriam when the Lord punishes her for attacking him.

❑ *Numbers 13:1-33.* From their location south of Palestine, the Israelites send out explorers to see whether an attempt to enter the land from the south is practical. They spy out the hill country around Hebron, south of Jerusalem. This territory figured prominently in the stories of the ancestors, particularly Abraham.

The explorers return with a mixed report. The land is all they expected but its inhabitants are fearsome and have a strong defense. Caleb, prominent elsewhere in Israel's conquest of Canaan (Joshua 14:6-14), is the only one who thinks they can conquer the land.

❏ *Numbers 14:1- 45.* The people resume their complaining and express their longing for Egypt. Notice the similarity of their complaints here with those in Chapter 11 and Exodus 16.

Joshua and Caleb try to prevent the people from going back to Egypt. They urge them to go up into the land of Canaan. However, the people choose to live by their fears and even go so far as to threaten the lives of the two courageous explorers.

What follows is an interesting exchange between the Lord, who in anger had decided to destroy Israel, and Moses, who again intercedes and pleads for the people's survival. Moses points out that the destruction of Israel will reflect on God's power to bring them into the Promised Land. Furthermore, such action is not in keeping with God's steadfast love.

God relents on the point of immediate destruction, but determines that no one who was delivered from Egypt and who has now rejected God will enter Canaan. Those of the next generation will inherit the Promised Land at the conclusion of forty years of desert wandering. Only the faithful Caleb and Joshua are excluded from this decree.

DIMENSION THREE:
WHAT DOES THE BIBLE MEAN TO ME?

Numbers 10:1-10—God's People on the Move

God's command to Moses to make two silver trumpets seems to have little to do with our life today. The key word, however, is *memorial* in verse 10. The trumpets are the means by which later Israelites are to recapture and remember the flavor and meaning of their ancestors' pilgrimage.

One of the purposes of worship in any generation is to bring to mind the church's past experience. What do we commemorate? What symbols aid remembrance of our beginnings as the church?

Numbers 10:11-28—Order in Our Lives

Israel's journey from Sinai finally begins. The details of Chapters 1–9 now take on full meaning. They are preparation for the march.

Using the biblical image, we sometimes speak of the church as a pilgrim people. These early chapters in Numbers remind us of the need for structure, definition, and worship. Yet structure, definition, and worship are only the basis for our mission, our moving out.

What things in the life of the church help order our life as the people of God? What structures and definitions do we need? How do we keep these structures and definitions from becoming objects of comfort and security to such a degree that we lose our sense of mission?

Numbers 11:1-6—The Problems of Freedom

Israel's desert wandering is filled with almost continuous complaining about problems and difficulties. Delivered from the oppression of Egypt, the Hebrews flinch before the hardships that accompany freedom. They wish they were back in Egypt where they had eaten well!

Growth is sometimes a painful process. Longing for freedom from restrictions, we often do not take into account the price of freedom. The Bible reminds us that God wills freedom and abhors the forces of oppression. However, with freedom comes the responsibility to handle problems and make decisions in a mature way.

It is important that we identify the comfortable places in our lives that keep us from growing. What pulls us back to Egypt? What securities keep us from responding to God's leading?

The church may also be enslaved by comfortable surroundings. Where have we failed to speak out against oppression? Where have we been fearful and faithless and left our mission undone?

Numbers 11:10-17, 24-30; 12:1-16—A Leadership Model

Even a great leader like Moses needed help. God provided this help by empowering the seventy elders to share the burden with him.

In the New Testament, Luke's story of Jesus' sending out of the seventy-two (Luke 10:1-11) may be related to this account in Numbers. In Luke's account, however, the seventy-two are to spread the gospel.

The Moses story suggests that the most effective form of leadership is that which is shared. At what point do we need this kind of leadership today? What are the characteristics of shared leadership?

Aaron and Miriam's struggle with Moses brings up another aspect of leadership—the leader's uniqueness. Moses emerges as having a particular immediacy in his relation with God. The full view of leadership must include both commitment to sharing and awareness of one's unique gifts.

What does this example say to our models of leadership in the church today? How are leaders to relate to one another?

Numbers 13:1-33—Realism, Faith, and the Future

The Bible's best-known spy story tells us that the explorers all went to the same place and experienced the same things. Their description of Canaan includes desirable and undesirable elements. Yet Caleb disagrees with the rest of the explorers about what Israel should do. What is the difference? What did Caleb see that the others did not?

Current events and conditions lead some to a daring faith and others to a shrinking fear. Where do you see evidences of this faith and fear in the church today? What does our Christian faith have to do with our understanding of the world and our attitude toward the future?

Aaron's staff . . . had not only sprouted but had budded,
blossomed and produced almonds (17:8).

— 4 —
The Perilous
Journey Continues
Numbers 15–21

DIMENSION ONE:
WHAT DOES THE BIBLE SAY?

Answer these questions by reading Numbers 15

1. What is to accompany Israel's animal offerings? (15:1-11)

2. When the people sin unintentionally, what is the community to do? (15:22-25)

3. How is the community to treat the man who gathers sticks on the sabbath? (15:32-36)

4. Why are the Israelites to wear tassels on the corners of their garments? (15:37-40)

Answer these questions by reading Numbers 16

5. What charge do Korah and his supporters bring against Moses and Aaron? What does Moses tell the Korahites to do? (16:1-3, 16-19)

6. Why are Dathan and Abiram punished, and what happens to them? (16;12-15, 25-33)

7. How does God punish the Korahites? (16:20-24, 35)

8. When the Lord punishes Israel for her constant grumbling, what keeps the plague from destroying all of Israel? (16:41-48)

Answer this question by reading Numbers 17

9. How does the Lord make known his choice of Aaron? (17:1-11)

Answer these questions by reading Numbers 18

10. Since the priests have no inheritance, what is their portion? (18:8-20)

11. What do the Levites receive? (18:21-24)

Answer these questions by reading Numbers 19

12. How do the priests produce the ashes that are used in the water for impurity? (19:1-9)

13. Who is unclean, and how are they cleansed? (19:14-19)

Answer these questions by reading Numbers 20

14. Where is Miriam buried? (20:1)

15. After the people are given water from a rock at Meribah, what judgment does the Lord pronounce on Moses and Aaron? (20:2-13)

16. What do the Israelites request of the king of Edom, and what is his answer? (20:14-21)

17. When Aaron dies, who succeeds him? How is this signified? (20:23-29)

Answer these questions by reading Numbers 21

18. What happens when the people complain against God and Moses? (21:4-6) What saves them? (21:7-9)

19. What king do the Israelites defeat, and what territory do they occupy as a result? (21:21-30)

20. What other king do they defeat? (21:33-35)

DIMENSION TWO:
WHAT DOES THE BIBLE MEAN?

❑ *Numbers 15:1-16.* As mentioned earlier, the Book of Numbers is a mixture of story and regulation. Following the story of the explorers, Chapter 15 is devoted mainly to regulation.

The phrase "an aroma pleasing to the LORD" in verses 3, 7, 10, and 13 is similar to Genesis 8:21, which tells of Noah's sacrifice after the Flood. Although this phrase sounds strange to us, it is the writer's way of saying that the sacrifices are acceptable.

The New International Version of the Bible does not translate the measures used. An *ephah* is a dry measure of about three-fifths of a bushel; and a *hin* is a liquid measure of about four quarts or four liters.

❑ *Numbers 15:22-31.* Persons may break the commandments inadvertently. In such cases, proper offering brings forgiveness. Persons cannot atone for conscious, deliberate breaking of the commandments. The person who "sins defiantly" must be removed from the community.

❑ *Numbers 15:37-41.* The wearing of tassels had significance for other peoples in the ancient world. Texts from Mari in upper Mesopotamia, dated in the eighteenth century B.C., refer to the use of tassels along with locks of hair as representations of a person. Within Israel's covenant religion, however, the tassel serves as a reminder to observe the commandments, and thus avoid inadvertent sin. In New Testament times, the Pharisee was noted for wearing tassels.

❑ *Numbers 16:41-50.* The people murmur against Moses and Aaron again—this time because of the death of the Korahites. Moses instructs Aaron to make atonement for the people with a filled censer, the only instance of atonement through use of incense recorded in the Old Testament.

The Hebrew word for *atonement* is *kaphar,* meaning "to cover." Atonement is understood as covering over or erasing sin rather than placating divine wrath.

❑ *Numbers 18:21-24.* The Levites are supported by the tithe, a tenth of agricultural products. In Deuteronomy 14:28-29, the tithe of every third year is shared among the Levites, widows, orphans, and resident aliens. Probably the regulation changed over the years, so that in later times, the Levites received all of the tithe every year, as specified here.

❑ *Numbers 19:1-22.* The ritual of the red heifer is unusual. The animal is not killed on the altar, although it is for the removal of sin. The blood of the animal is burned with the rest of the carcass, a practice that differs from the standard custom.

❑ *Numbers 20:1-13.* The events of this section take place thirty-eight years after those of the previous chapters. The death of Aaron, recounted in verses 22-29, is dated by Numbers 33:38 in the fortieth year after leaving Egypt. The opening chapter of Numbers picks up the second year of their sojourn in the desert.

Verse 1 tells of the death of Miriam, sister of Moses and Aaron. Although she appears infrequently, she is important in the tradition. She is regarded as a prophetess, renowned for leading the celebration of their deliverance at the sea with her song of victory (Exodus 15:20-21). Numbers 12 recounts her participation with Aaron in a challenge to Moses. Later generations spoke of her as one of the three leaders of the desert journey (Micah 6:4).

Kadesh is a large oasis in the desert that lies to the south of Canaan. Kadesh was probably the center of Israel's activity during the desert sojourn. In Numbers 13, the explorers went out from Kadesh for their journey into Canaan.

Verses 2-13 of Chapter 20 recount still another event in the complaint tradition. The nature of Moses' sin has drawn much speculation. Some interpreters believe that he doubts God's power. Others suggest that he claims credit for the miracle, and still others think that his impatience with the people brings God's judgment. The Hebrew verb used in verse 3 is *rib,* which means "to contend." The name of the place (verse 13) is *Meribah,* which comes from the same root and means "contention."

❑ *Numbers 20:14-21.* The Israelites now begin the final stage of their journey. They start out in a wide circle to the east. This route brings them to Edom, but the Edomite king refuses them passage through his territory.

❑ *Numbers 21:10-20.* The geography of Israel's movements at this point is difficult to describe clearly. According to this account, Israel moved south around Edom and proceeded up the western side of Edom, turning east at the boundary brook Zered in order to circle Moab. When they reached the Arnon River, they moved northwestward into the territory of the Amorites. The Amorites lived east of the Jordan between the Arnon and Jabbok Rivers.

DIMENSION THREE:
WHAT DOES THE BIBLE MEAN TO ME?

Numbers 15:1-31—The Abundance of Offerings

The Israelites believe that the God of history has made a covenant with them. Their acts of worship are a response to this belief. They bring offerings to a God who has already established his relationship with them. The offerings fulfill and maintain that relationship.

How do we respond in our worship to God's covenant? What channel do we have to express devotion and loyalty?

Israel's worship does not provide an offering for intentional sins. The sin offering deals with mistakes—unintended breaches of the commandments of God. Yet, are they not excusable without recourse to sacrifices? Should we be concerned with mistakes? What are we as Christians called to do about our mistakes?

Suppose a driver is preoccupied, goes through a red traffic light, and causes a personal injury accident. What in the Christian faith can help this person deal with the results of this mistake? What resources do Christians have for dealing with the guilt and pain of others?

Numbers 16—Crisis in Leadership

Struggles in leadership can develop in any organization or movement. The challenges from Korah, Dathan, and Abiram challenge both Moses' religious authority and his political leadership.

THE PERILOUS JOURNEY CONTINUES   **33**

What causes conflict in leadership? What criteria help determine a leader's fitness? How do we distinguish between self-glorification and use of one's position for the common good?

If you had been present, would you have supported Korah? Dathan and Abiram?

Numbers 19:1-10—The Red Heifer

The strange ritual of the red heifer is meant to provide purification from uncleanness, particularly contact with the dead. Hebrews 9:13-14 gives a New Testament interpretation. These verses point to the superiority of Christ's sacrifice over the ashes of the heifer in the act of purification. Saint Augustine, early in the fifth century, interpreted Numbers 19 allegorically. For him the victim symbolizes Christ; the red color is the blood of the passion. The cedar wood represents hope; the hyssop, faith; and the scarlet, charity. The dead that produce uncleanness are dead works.

Although many rightly question Augustine's extensive allegorizing, Augustine points to the underlying concern of the passage—purification from disabling uncleanness. The idea of what defiles has changed throughout religious history. Defilement in human experience cannot be doubted, however, and the concern for its removal is important.

What provision does the church make for cleansing? How does this cleansing appear in our worship? What part of the gospel speaks specifically to our need for cleansing?

Numbers 21:4-9—The Bronze Snake

The account of the snake in the desert has had an interesting history. In the ancient world, snakes were believed to have magical power that promoted healing and rejuvenation. For Israel, however, the snake has only the power that God gives it.

In 2 Kings 18:4, Hezekiah removes Moses' bronze snake from the Temple because people are burning incense to it. As mentioned earlier, John 3:14 refers to Moses' lifting up the snake in the desert and compares it to Jesus' being lifted up on the cross and thus making eternal life available.

What thread runs through all of these accounts and interpretations? How does it enrich our Christian understanding of God and the divine action in Jesus Christ?

Numbers 21:10-35—From Preparation to Action

A new era is beginning for Israel. The older generation, condemned to wander in the desert, is passing away. Israel's story turns toward the Conquest of Canaan.

Often all the activity in our lives and in the life of the church seems to be meaningless—a wandering without purpose. The story of Israel tells us this is not so. The people of God move through the testing of the desert to fulfillment in the Promised Land. What uncertainties and anxieties from your desert appear in life today? What lessons from your desert should we heed in our journey? What signs of promise does the Christian faith hold for us?

I brought you to curse my enemies, but you have done nothing but bless them! (23:11).

— 5 —

Balaam and the Moabites

Numbers 22–27

DIMENSION ONE: WHAT DOES THE BIBLE SAY?

Answer these questions by reading Numbers 22

1. What is the Moabite reaction to the Israelites? (22:1-3)

2. Why does Balak send for Balaam? (22:4-6)

3. Why won't Balaam come at first? (22:7-13)

4. What is the Lord's instruction when he allows Balaam to go? (22:15-20)

5. How is Balaam's life saved as he travels? (22:21-35)

6. When Balaam arrives in Moab, on what condition will he speak? (22:36-38)

Answer these questions by reading Numbers 23

7. Does Balaam curse the Israelites for Balak? What does Balaam say about them? (23:1-10)

8. In his second oracle, what does Balaam say about God's relationship to Israel? (23:18-24)

Answer these questions by reading Numbers 24

9. What is Balaam's vision of Israel's future? (24:3-9)

10. How does Balak respond to Balaam's vision? (24:10-11)

11. How does Balaam's fourth oracle describes the future relationship between Moab and Israel? What does it say? (24:15-17)

Answer these questions by reading Numbers 25

12. What does Israel do to deserve God's punishment? (25:1-5)

13. What is Phinehas's reward for his bold action against Zimri and Cozbi? (25:6-15)

Answer these questions by reading Numbers 26

14. What are the census totals for each tribe listed below? (26:1-50)

Reuben	_____	Manasseh	_____
Simeon	_____	Ephraim	_____
Gad	_____	Benjamin	_____
Judah	_____	Dan	_____
Issachar	_____	Asher	_____
Zebulun	_____	Naphtali	_____

15. How many people from the first census are counted in the later one? (26:63-65)

Answer these questions by reading Numbers 27

16. What decision is reached concerning the inheritance of Zelophehad's five daughters? (27:1-11)

17. Whom does the Lord select as Moses' successor? What is Moses to do to him? (27:12-19)

DIMENSION TWO:
WHAT DOES THE BIBLE MEAN?

❑ *Numbers 22:1.* Following the victories over the Amorites and Og, king of Bashan, Israel moves to the plains of Moab—the final encampment before entering Canaan. The reference is to a plain some five to seven miles wide on the east side of the Jordan just north of the Dead Sea.

❑ *Numbers 22:2-20.* Fearful of Israel, the Moabites summon Balaam, a famous seer with powers of blessing and cursing. The story of the negotiation between Balaam and Balak's agents revolves around Balaam's understanding of the Lord's will. It is surprising to note that Balaam, a non-Israelite, consults Israel's God. The story implies that anything affecting Israel would necessarily involve Israel's God.

❑ *Numbers 22:21-35.* In verse 22, the NIV uses the word *oppose* while the NRSV uses *adversary* to translate the Hebrew word *satan.* In the Old Testament, *satan* is understood to be a member of God's heavenly council, the tester of faith (Job 1–2), or persecutor (Zechariah 3). In the intertestamental period (200 B.C.–A.D. 100), Satan comes to be understood as the prince of evil.

When Balaam's eyes are opened, and he understands that his way is blocked by the angel of the Lord, he assumes he should return home. The angel, however, tells him to proceed to Moab but to speak only what God tells him to say.

Why does the Lord stop him on the way when he had already given Balaam permission to go? Most interpreters suggest that these verses emphasize the point that God is in control, and Balaam must say what God tells him to say.

❑ *Numbers 22:41–23:12.* The first oracle sets forth Balaam's dilemma. Balak expects Balaam, a seer renowned for his special powers in cursing, to use these powers against Israel. However, God is in control. Whatever power curses and blessings have is subject to divine will.

Balaam recognizes Israel's special place among the nations. Verse 10 notes the multitude of the people, a mark of blessing. The "fourth part" in the second line is better read as "dust clouds."

❑ *Numbers 23:19-26.* The second oracle emphasizes the un-changeable nature of God's good purposes concerning Israel. "Son of man" in the second line parallels "man" in the first line, and both terms indicate human mortality.

God has brought the Israelites out of Egypt and has made them a strong and fierce people. "The strength of a wild ox" (verse 22) is a figure of speech for the great power of God as manifested in Israel's deliverance from Egypt. Against this power, Balaam cannot invoke a curse.

❑ *Numbers 23:27–24:9.* At Peor, a third site, Balak asks Balaam again to curse Israel. The Spirit of God comes upon him. (See 1 Samuel 10:5-6, 10-11; 19:23-24 for similar experiences.) In his vision of the future, Balaam sees Israel as a powerful nation that will overcome its enemies. The oracle closes with the words of blessing found in God's promise to Abraham in Genesis 12:3.

❑ *Numbers 24:10-19.* Dismissed by Balak, Balaam volunteers a fourth oracle. In the distant future he sees a figure who will arise out of Israel to crush Moab and Edom. The symbols for this figure are "star" and "scepter" (verse 17). The figure mentioned here has been variously identified as David; an unnamed, expected messiah; Bar Kokhba, leader of a revolt against Rome in A.D. 132–135, and Jesus. Whatever identifica-tion is given in later interpretation, the original reference is clearly to a king who will lead Israel in bringing Moab and Edom to submission.

❑ *Numbers 25:1-5.* Immediately after Balaam's blessing, the Israelites become involved in illicit sexual activity with the Moabites. This activity draws them into the worship of Baal of Peor. The prophet Hosea considers this event a turning point in Israel's life (Hosea 9:10). In Hosea's view, the children of Israel enjoy a unique relationship to the Lord until they become involved with the fertility deity at Peor. Afterwards the relationship is changed.

❑ *Numbers 26:1-65.* The second census, taken in preparation for entry into Canaan, follows the same tribal order as Chapter 2, except for the reversal of Ephraim and Manasseh. The second list has some differences in form, however. Clan infor-mation is added in the second generation names. The list extends the references to Reuben, Judah, Manasseh, and Asher even further.

❑ *Numbers 27:1-11.* The story of Zelophehad's five daughters is a legal narrative like those of 9:6-14 and 15:32-36. In such accounts, a situation raises a question for which there is no precedent. Moses brings the case before God, who gives a divine word of decision. This word becomes the basis for all similar cases. In this case, inheritance rights are given to daughters where there are no sons in the family.

DIMENSION THREE:
WHAT DOES THE BIBLE MEAN TO ME?

Numbers 22–24—A King's Will and God's Purposes

The Balaam story is the longest in Numbers. This account tells of a king's employment of a famous seer to combat the threat of Israel. It unfolds around the seer's attempts to curse Israel in the face of God's blessing. The theme of the story is the conflict between the Lord's intention and the powers that seek to thwart the divine purpose.

On the surface, we read about conflict of nation with nation, oppression by the powerful, and headstrong willfulness of human leaders. However, another dimension of the story is God's carrying out of his purposes in history. The biblical story portrays the continuing tension between human ways of understanding and using power, and the belief that God is the ultimate lord of human history.

How can weak, enslaved Israel hope to win freedom over mighty Pharaoh's objections? How can Israel stand against the curses of the skillful and renowned Balaam? The Bible insists that the wrongful intentions of human pride cannot prevail against the purposes of the God of history.

Does the Bible present matters too simply? Do we really believe that a universal God of good will is functioning in our time? If so, what evidence supports this belief? In a world of terrorism, racism, and poverty, where is the God of justice and deliverance?

Perhaps the first question we need to ask is, On which side of the story do we find ourselves? Are we the people of God or the enslavers of God's people? Or are we both?

Where are we called to commit our voices and our efforts in light of our tradition that God works on the side of the oppressed? How does the Balaam story speak to the faith with which we work for justice and freedom?

Numbers 25:1-5—Realism and Faith

Israel is upheld by the power of God who turns curses to blessings. But Israel's internal affairs are not in line with God's will. The bubble of great expectations bursts! The people of God—with opportunity before them—get involved with the fertility religion of Moab. The Moabites were the very people who wanted to destroy them. So often in history, a country that can withstand external threats of major dimension succumbs to internal decay.

The biblical writers are aware of the human condition at this point. Immediately after Abraham's call (Genesis 12:1-8), we learn that he misrepresents his relationship with Sarah to avoid danger. God preserves Noah and his family because Noah is a righteous man. Yet as soon as the Flood is over, we have the account in Genesis 9:20-27 where drunkenness and family division prevail. In this passage from Numbers, God's people abandon their God for the rites of the baalistic cult. Baal Peor signifies Israel's unfaithfulness.

The belief that God is at work in human experience is not a sweetness-and-light faith. The biblical story is not based on a naive God who is unaware of what human beings are really like. Israel's story gives us both the glorious vision and the grim reality of human existence. Yet it insists that God's purposes are at work through it all!

Where do we need such realism? What effect does it have on our faith? How can the reality of human existence affect our morale when we meet failure in ourselves?

Numbers 26—From One Generation to Another

A census is taken at both the beginning and the end of the desert experience. The one in Chapter 26 almost duplicates the Sinai census in Chapter 2. The second census is not merely repetition, however. It has a meaning of its own.

The key to the full meaning of the second census is in the final three verses. In the nearly forty years between the two, a new generation of Israelites has arisen. None of those numbered in the first census are present for the second.

Every great movement has a crisis point. This crisis arises when all the original participants die. The continuation of the movement depends on the first generation's ability to communicate its faith so that the next generation commits itself to the same degree.

The people of the new generation are far from perfect, but they are also the people of God. They live on in the vision that called their parents out of Egypt. They are now ready for the next big step. The experience of their parents has become the destiny of the following generations.

The question of continuity is important for us. What in the life of the Israelites has enabled them to continue from one generation to another? What factors have contributed to the stability of the church through the centuries? What practices, what action of God, what resources, what kind of faith have made this continuity possible?

What is our responsibility for continuing our faith? How can the church help us continue our faith from generation to generation? Can worship help? outreach? awareness of tradition? faith in God's action in history? covenant understanding?

These are the commands and regulations the LORD gave through Moses (36:13).

— 6 —

Preparing for The Promised Land

Numbers 28–36

DIMENSION ONE:
WHAT DOES THE BIBLE SAY?

Answer these questions by reading Numbers 28

1. What animal offerings are the people to make daily? What is to accompany these? (28:3-5, 7)

2. For what other occasions does the Lord specify offerings? (28:9, 11, 16-19, 26)

Answer these questions by reading Numbers 29

3. In addition to the two sacred assemblies mentioned in Chapter 28 (verses 18, 26), what three occasions call for sacred assembly in Israel's religious calendar? (29:1, 7, 12)

4. How long does the third festival last? How does it end? (29:12-38)

Answer these questions by reading Numbers 30

5. How does the vow of a woman still in her father's house differ from that of a man? (30:1-5)

6. How does marriage affect a woman's vows? (30:6-8, 10-12)

7. How do widowhood and divorce affect a woman's vows? (30:9)

Answer these questions by reading Numbers 31

8. Against whom do the Israelites go to war? (31:1-2) What is the outcome? (31:7-11)

9. Whose counsel does Moses blame for Israel's sin at Peor? (31:16) What happens to the one blamed? (31:8)

10. How are the spoils from the battle with the Midianites divided? (31:25-32) What levies does Moses take from each half? (31:28-30)

Answer these questions by reading Numbers 32

11. What tribes ask for land east of the Jordan? (32:1-5)

12. What do they agree to do before settling down? (32:6-7, 16-27)

Answer this question by reading Numbers 33

13. What is (1) the starting point of Israel's journey, (2) some of its most memorable stopping points, and (3) the location of the final encampment before Canaan? (33:5, 8, 15, 36-37, 48)

Answer these questions by reading Numbers 34

14. What information does God relay to Moses? (34:1-12)

15. How many tribes does Moses include in the division of the land of Canaan? (34:13-15)

Answer these questions by reading Numbers 35

16. What is Israel to provide for the Levites? (35:1-8)

17. What purpose do the cities of refuge serve? (35:9-15)

18. What is the distinction between a murderer and one who is to be spared from the avenger of blood? (35:16-28)

Answer this question by reading Numbers 36

19. Why must the daughters of Zelophehad marry within their own tribe? (36:1-9)

DIMENSION TWO:
WHAT DOES THE BIBLE MEAN?

❏ *Numbers 28:1-8.* The list of offerings begins with the basic element in the system, the daily offering. Each animal offering is accompanied by grain and drink offerings. The drink offering is to be poured out "at the sanctuary," that is, at the base of the altar.

❏ *Numbers 28:16-25.* The first of Israel's main festivals, the one in early spring, combines the Passover and the Feast of Unleavened Bread. The former involves no offerings, because it is essentially a family observance. The Feast of Unleavened

Bread runs for seven days with a full set of offerings each day. The first and last days are marked by a "sacred assembly." On these days, work ceases, and the people gather.

❏ *Numbers 28:26-31.* The required offerings here are the same as those for the Feasts of the New Moon and Unleavened Bread. The festival falls at the beginning of the wheat harvest, hence the reference to first fruits.

❏ *Numbers 29:1-11.* Most regulations pertaining to Israel's fall festival mention only the Feast of Booths. Here two other holy days precede that festival. The first day of the seventh month is a special day, marked by holy convocation, special offerings, and a blowing of trumpets. This day is still observed as the Jewish New Year.

The words "deny yourselves" (verse 7) and "sin offering for atonement" (verse 11) mark the observance ten days later of Yom Kippur, the day of atonement.

❏ *Numbers 28:12-38.* Elsewhere called the Feast of Ingathering or Booths, this major fall festival celebrates the end of the fruit and olive harvest.

❏ *Numbers 30:1-16.* The vow is a serious and important matter in ancient times. The patriarchal structure of Israelite society makes a woman's vow subject to the authority of father or husband. However, the disapproval of the father or husband must be expressed at once, or the vow is valid.

❏ *Numbers 31:1-24.* The war of vengeance against the Midianites is a religious war. Phinehas, the priest, leads it, and the vessels from the sanctuary are taken into battle.

Balaam is among the slain Midianites (verse 8). He is also set forth as the one whose counsel to the Midianite women led to Israel's unfaithfulness at Peor (verse 16). This picture—rather than the more favorable one in Chapters 22–24—is the basis for the negative New Testament references to Balaam in Jude 11 and Revelation 2:14.

❏ *Numbers 32:1-5.* Two of the tribes ask to settle down between the Arnon and Jabbok Rivers, an area Israel had obtained by defeating Sihon (Numbers 21:21-24). Heshbon, roughly in the center of the area concerned, is about sixteen miles northeast of the point where the Jordan enters the Dead Sea.

❏ *Numbers 33:50-56.* As the people pass over into Canaan, they are to rid the land of all Canaanites. By doing so, they can avoid compromise with the Canaanite religion. This emphasis on pagan religions is central to the Book of Deuteronomy, which focuses on loyalty to the Lord. The figured stones, molten images, and high places are all well-known elements of baalism.

❏ *Numbers 35:9-28.* In ancient times, the altar served as sanctuary in many cultures. A person pursued by an avenger could claim divine protection, and thus delay vengeance until passions cooled. The cities of refuge are to provide such protection when local shrines with their altars are inaccessible.

The cities of refuge protect only those involved in accidental killing. The slayer must stay in the city until the high priest dies, and then he may return home without danger. Apparently, the death of a national leader (the high priest) brings expiation for the slaying.

❏ *Numbers 36:1-12.* The decision concerning Zelophehad's daughters (Numbers 27:1-11) relates to the social value of tribal landholding. A woman's inheritance follows her into marriage as she goes to the family of her husband. Thus, the original tribe suffers a decrease in land if she marries outside her tribe. The regulation that emerges is meant to prevent such a loss.

DIMENSION THREE:
WHAT DOES THE BIBLE MEAN TO ME?

Numbers 28:16-31; 29:1-16, 35-38—Festival and Offering

The life and worship of Israel cannot be understood fully unless we understand the meaning of their festival celebrations. The festivals include the recital of God's saving acts and the meaning of the covenant relationship extended to Israel. The emphasis is on a remembrance that is more than simple recall of past facts. Remembrance in celebration is the Israelites' way of reminding themselves who they are and what God has done for them. It is also a time for the regular renewal of covenant relationship and commitment.

This section of Numbers emphasizes the offering required for each of the festivals. The underlying purpose of the offerings is a concern for full and regular service to God.

In our Judeo-Christian tradition, festivals (particularly Christmas, Easter, and Pentecost) play an important part in our sense of identity and our participation in the church. How does this section of Numbers speak to us? How do we respond to God's action in Christ as we celebrate our festivals? What offerings represent our service to God?

Numbers 31:1-20; 33:55-56
The Dilemma of God's People

We have difficulty dealing with a God who destroys whole peoples and blesses Israel's national interests against all others. However, the Scripture's purpose is not to focus on God. It addresses the ever-present question of how to be God's people in the midst of peoples with a different view of God and life. The question for Israel is not how to make everyone believe as she does, but how to be true to the covenant with a righteous God. As Christians, what challenges do we face while living as God's people in a diverse culture? How can we meet these challenges?

The Peor incident threatens Israel's identity and sense of purpose in history. After Israel enters the Promised Land, the Canaanites represent the same threat to their existence and mission as the people of God.

One of the Old Testament answers to this threat is the one found here. It emphasizes the difference between loyalty to Israel's God and to all other ways of life. Israel reminds us of the importance of being clear about our ethical and moral decisions—both personally and corporately. In what ways can we live dedicated Christian lives, compatible with our view of God's universal love?

Numbers 32:1-7, 16-27—Following Through

The tribes of Reuben and Gad (and later part of Manasseh) want the territory east of the Jordan. They ask Moses to let them settle there, saying, "Do not make us cross the Jordan."

Moses' strong reaction to this request reflects a fundamental Old Testament concept—the wholeness of the people of God. Are the tribes of Reuben and Gad to be allowed to settle here, leaving the others to go on, reduced in strength? Can one group claim its rewards early and withdraw from the common endeavor? To allow these tribes to withdraw would demoralize the rest of Israel.

Have you been involved in an endeavor that failed because persons withdrew their support? How did those who remained feel about those who withdrew? Where are we called to follow through with our commitments for the sake of the whole group? What does the idea of following through say about our commitment to the church?

Numbers 35:9-34—Murder and Society

Israel's approach to the killing of a human being involved three elements: the avenger, the cities of refuge, and the belief that spilled blood corrupts the land.

Numbers 35 attempts to put these three ideas together in some kind of workable combination. Israel never takes slaying lightly or loses its sense of the divine value of human life. At the same time, Israel makes provision for distinction of motive. The defilement of the land is expiated by the blood of the murderer or the death of the high priest.

What does Israel's double concern for the seriousness of killing and the protection of the rights of the accidental slayer say to us? What is the implication of expiation without taking the life of the killer? How can the ideas in this passage help us develop ways to bring wholeness into a society injured by murder? What does this passage say to Christians who are discussing capital punishment for the crime of murder?

PREPARING FOR THE PROMISED LAND   **51**

Numbers 36:1-12—Freedom and Limitation

The decision in Chapter 27 about inheritance by daughters conflicts with Israel's strong commitment to tribal landholding. Given the social structure in which a woman joins her husband's family, the way is now open for tribes to lose part of their land to other tribes. The result is that a new freedom—the right of daughters to inherit—is restricted by new regulations about marriage.

Within a social system, change and greater openness often raise new questions. In our time of growing social sensitivity, we also face problems and questions resulting from social change. What insights can we gain from the way Israel handled this case? What social and personal adjustments must we make to allow freedom for everyone?

These are the words Moses spoke to all Israel (1:1).

7

Moses Recounts God's Acts
Deuteronomy 1–3

DIMENSION ONE:
WHAT DOES THE BIBLE SAY?

Answer these questions by reading Deuteronomy 1

1. Where does Moses speak to all Israel? (1:1-5)

2. What does Moses report that God said at Horeb? (1:6-8)

3. Why does Moses appoint other leaders? (1:9-18)

4. What do the children of Israel ask Moses to do at Kadesh Barnea? (1:22-23)

5. Why do the Israelites refuse to go into the Promised Land? (1:26-28)

6. What is the Lord's reaction to their refusal? (1:34-40)

7. Why does Israel fail in the later attempt to fight the Amorites as the Lord commanded? (1:41-46)

Answer these questions by reading Deuteronomy 2

8. Who has given Seir to the descendants of Esau? (2:1-5)

9. What are the Israelites to do as they pass through Seir? (2:6)

10. Where do the Israelites go after this? How are they to treat the inhabitants there? (2:8-10)

11. With whom does Israel do battle? What is the result? (2:24-36)

12. What country does Israel avoid? (2:37)

Answer these questions by reading Deuteronomy 3

13. What is the result when Israel goes to war with Og of Bashan? (3:1-7)

14. Of what group is Og a remnant? What shows his size? (3:11)

15. To whom does Moses give the conquered territory? What does the half-tribe of Manasseh receive? (3:12-17)

16. What does Moses expect these tribes to do? (3:18-20)

DIMENSION TWO:
WHAT DOES THE BIBLE MEAN?

With this lesson we enter the fifth and final book of the Pentateuch. The Book of Deuteronomy gets its name from a Greek term meaning "second law." Even though the book portrays Moses as expanding the law, Deuteronomy does not pretend to be a second law. It is a continuation of the law of Sinai—an explanation given by Moses in his last days just before Israel enters Canaan.

❏ *Deuteronomy 1:1-8.* "These are the words Moses spoke," the opening clause of the Book of Deuteronomy, gives us the viewpoint of the whole book. The emphasis throughout Deuteronomy is on Moses as speaker. While Deuteronomy makes it clear that divine revelation lies behind Moses' words (verse 3), it is distinctive in its presentation of Moses as the preacher and interpreter of the law.

MOSES RECOUNTS GOD'S ACTS   **55**

The audience is "all Israel," which reflects another Deuteronomic emphasis—the unity of Israel. The phrase, "in the desert east of the Jordan," indicates clearly that those who wrote Deuteronomy were located in Canaan (the west side of the Jordan).

Moses' speech begins with a summary of the historical events that Israel had experienced between Horeb and the present encampment. *Horeb* is the name used in Deuteronomy for the place called Sinai in other Old Testament passages.

Moses associates the promise of the land with God's covenant made to the patriarchs (verse 8). In the Book of Deuteronomy, Israel is seen as living between the ancient promise of the land and the fulfillment that is to come with the possession of Canaan.

❑ *Deuteronomy 1:9-18.* It is not clear whether Moses appoints one or two sets of leaders. These leaders clearly have military responsibilities. The qualifications given in verse 13 imply that they function as judges also. However, verses 16-18 direct a set of instructions to "judges." These instructions suggest a separate group. In any case, Moses asks for aid in the heavy task of leadership. He reorganizes and delegates responsibility.

❑ *Deuteronomy 1:19-46.* The explorers' story is familiar to us from Numbers 13–14. While both accounts describe Israel's faithlessness, the one in Deuteronomy highlights certain elements in a different way. In Deuteronomy, when told the land is before them for their taking, the people ask that explorers be sent. In Numbers 13, the Lord initiates this step. The explorers' report is much briefer and more positive in Deuteronomy. The doubt of the people in refusing to go into Canaan receives primary attention. Deuteronomy emphasizes Israel's fear and anxiety about the Lord's ability to fulfill the promise of land.

In the account of the Meribah event of Numbers 20:2-13, God judges Moses for his own sin. In Deuteronomy 1:37, however, Moses attributes that judgment to the fact that Israel refused to believe the Lord and enter Canaan. Israel's lack of faith is behind Deuteronomy's strong emphasis on the unity of Israel as a people.

❏ *Deuteronomy 2:1-8.* Israel passes through Seir on the way to Canaan. This passage reminds us of the story in Numbers 20:14-21, but again Deuteronomy's emphasis is different. The Deuteronomy account does not refuse permission to pass through as the previous story. The Lord tells them to avoid conflict with the sons of Esau, whom the Old Testament calls Edomites. God has given the Edomites their land and will not allow Israel to violate their territory. God acts in history for Israel's neighbors as well as for Israel.

❏ *Deuteronomy 2:26-37.* Conditions change when the Israelites cross the Arnon and enter the territory of King Sihon. They approach him on the same terms as they did the Edomites, Moabites, and Ammonites. But he refuses to cooperate. Sihon's obstinacy is part of divine providence (verse 30). His stubbornness clears the way for Israel to overcome him and take his territory.

The verb used for "completely destroyed" in verse 34 denotes the use of the ban. The ban involves total destruction of people, cities, and property as a way of devoting (that is, sacrificing) everything to the deity who gives the victory.

❏ *Deuteronomy 3:1-11.* Bashan is a rich grazing area north of Gilead. The meaning of its name in Hebrew is "fertile."

These chapters provide explanatory notes on places and peoples. One of these "footnotes" (verse 11) refers to Og as a remnant of the Rephaim. Rephaimites were legendary early inhabitants of Canaan usually remembered for their large size. The footnote goes on to record the size of Og's bedstead. The size—thirteen feet by six feet—supports the memory of Og as the last of the giants.

❏ *Deuteronomy 3:12-22.* As in Numbers 32, these tribes are to join the other tribes in the conquest of Canaan, "until the LORD gives rest to your brothers" (verse 20). *Rest* is an important word in Deuteronomy. It means more than physical relaxation or peace of mind. Its full meaning points to the peace that Israel will gain when the people occupy the Promised Land, have a home of their own, and are free from the precarious life of wandering.

❏ *Deuteronomy 3:23-29.* Moses pleads to be allowed to enter Canaan. He wants to see the climax of the story, the fullness of God's action. But the Lord is angry with him on Israel's account. Moses, as part of Israel, is accountable for the common faithlessness.

The view from Pisgah is all God allows Moses to see. But this view may be more significant than supposed. In ancient times, the legal transfer of property took place when the new owner looked it over (Genesis 13:14-17).

After all their wandering, the final verse of the historical introduction locates the Israelites at Baal Peor. Baal Peor is the place where Israel first encountered the fertility cult (Numbers 25:3; Deuteronomy 4:3). Here Israel will be given the regulations for life as the covenant people of God.

DIMENSION THREE:
WHAT DOES THE BIBLE MEAN TO ME?

Deuteronomy 1:1—Moses and God's Revelation

"These are the words Moses spoke to all Israel." With its first words the Book of Deuteronomy shows its uniqueness. The preceding books speak of the Lord's instruction to Moses for Israel. Deuteronomy consists, almost entirely, of the words of Moses. The prominence of Moses' role is significant.

The audience is "all Israel," emphasizing the unity of Israel's people. Many references in the book indicate that this unity also refers to successive generations. Each generation is part of the people of God. God's revelation is always contemporary (Deuteronomy 5:1-5).

How is God's revelation to us similar to God's revelation to the people of Israel? How is it different? What role do men and women play in God's revelation? How important is the whole church to the perception of God's will?

Deuteronomy 1:19-33—Distorted Vision

Deuteronomy's version of the spy story highlights the people's failure to respond in faith to God's call for action. They conclude that they were brought out of Egypt and led to Canaan because the Lord hated them. Moses reminds them of the deliverance from Egypt and the desert experience in which God carried them as a father bears a son. In spite of all the signs of God's love, the people continue to view God as a hateful enemy.

Acting in faith—trusting divine providence as a basis for action—is not easy. Fear and anxiety exaggerate life's negative aspects and make trust difficult. The ultimate expression of this lack of trust is the distorted vision that makes God's grace appear threatening and destructive whenever it calls for responsive, risking action.

The meaning of events and conditions in our times is just as difficult to read. Where is the church today called to launch out in risky action? What signs of God's providence make this a sensible course of action? What events are we possibly misreading as threats when they are really opportunities if seen through the eyes of faith?

Deuteronomy 1:41-46—Living With the Consequences

When the Israelites become aware of God's punishment for their faithlessness (verses 34-39), they admit their mistake and determine to go up against the Canaanites. They want to rectify their error. They go on their own, even though Moses warns them that God is not with them. The result is utter defeat.

How are we to understand the frustration of the Israelites' attempt to right their wrong? The story seems to say that Israel, on her own, cannot reverse the consequences of her rebellious action. The course of history has moved past that point. The time is wrong. The call of God is to the future.

Opportunities ignored or refused are lost. This loss does not mean that the future is closed, but that a particular course of action has been closed, and its consequences are in place. Hope lies not in going back, but in facing the future with renewed faith.

How does this understanding affect our lives? What opportunities have we passed by and now cannot reclaim? How do faith and hope keep our lives open?

Deuteronomy 2:1-6, 8-9, 16-19—God and the Nation

Israel is not to contend with Edom, Moab, and Ammon. The Lord has given to each the territory it occupies. God's sovereignty over history and peoples is not confined to Israel's welfare. Israel's most difficult neighbors also occupy their lands by God's designation. Even as Deuteronomy focuses on Israel's life and destiny, it gives attention to the broader vistas of God's action in history.

How do national interests limit our sense of Christian responsibility? When our national interests clash with those of another nation, how can we ascertain God's will? Where do the aspirations of the peoples of developing countries fit into God's broader vista? Has God given them the right to their full place in world economics and politics?

Deuteronomy 3:23-28—Relinquishing Leadership

Moses makes one last plea to be allowed to go into Canaan. His petition grows out of his feeling that God's mighty acts have only begun. Until Israel possesses Canaan, the story is left unfinished. Moses wants to see the glorious outcome.

This vision is not to be. Moses is part of the old order. He shares in the communal guilt of Israel's faithlessness at Kadesh Barnea. God allows him to go up and look over into the land. Beyond that, however, he cannot go. Moses must entrust his concern for God's purposes with Israel to Joshua.

What understanding of leadership does this story give us? Where does this apply to church leadership today? Is limitation of tenure wise or wasteful? How are God's purposes best served?

I am the LORD your God, who brought you out of Egypt (5:6).

—— 8 ——

Moses Recalls the Covenant

Deuteronomy 4–5

DIMENSION ONE:
WHAT DOES THE BIBLE SAY?

Answer these questions by reading Deuteronomy 4

1. What is Israel to follow? for what purpose? (4:1)

2. Who survives Baal Peor? (4:3-4)

3. What two things does Israel have? (4:7-8)

4. When the Israelites stand at the foot of Mount Horeb, what does the Lord declare to them? (4:13)

5. Against what activities does Moses warn the Israelites? (4:15-19)

6. What will happen to Israel if the people makes idols? (4:25-28)

7. Will God forget the covenant? (4:29-31)

8. What two great things have happened to Israel? (4:32-35)

9. Where does Moses set the law before Israel? (4:44-46)

Answer these questions by reading Deuteronomy 5

10. With whom does God make the covenant at Horeb? (5:1-3)

11. Who gives these laws? (5:5-6)

12. What three commandments deal with God? (5:7-11)

13. Why is Israel to observe the sabbath? (5:12-15)

14. What is the result of honoring one's parents? (5:16)

15. The last five commandments concern human relationships. Summarize them by completing the sentence below. You shall not

(a)   (5:17)
(b)   (5:18)
(c)   (5:19)
(d)   (5:20)
(e)   (5:21)

16. What does the Lord tell Moses after the people go to their tents? (5:30-31)

DIMENSION TWO:
WHAT DOES THE BIBLE MEAN?

❑ *Deuteronomy 4:1-8.* The words "Hear now, O Israel" bring the hearers from reflecting on the past into the present. From this point on, Deuteronomy emphasizes the teaching that Moses gives Israel for life in the land of Canaan.

The phrase "the decrees and laws" uses two of Deuteronomy's favorite words. *Decree* translates the Hebrew word, *hoq,* which is translated in some other versions as "statute." *Law* is a translation of *mishpat,* a term that applies to judgments that are precedents. " That you may live . . . and take possession of the land" points to a fundamental teaching that obedience to the law leads to life while disobedience brings death.

❑ *Deuteronomy 4:9-14.* This passage links three terms, *Horeb, covenant,* and *ten commandments.* The first is the mountain of revelation. The mountain that Exodus calls Sinai, Deuteronomy calls Horeb. *Covenant* (first used in verse 13) is a central idea in Deuteronomy's thought. *Covenant* refers to the relationship between the Lord and Israel and the body of law that regulates that relationship.

❑ *Deuteronomy 4:15-24.* This discussion of idol worship picks up on a statement in verse 12. When the Israelite heard the

Lord at Mount Horeb, they "saw no form." On this basis, Moses warns Israel against making any image. The absence of images and idols in Israel's worship is unique among the religions of the ancient world.

❏ *Deuteronomy 4:25-31.* Calling "heaven and earth as witnesses" (verse 26) is a practice that also appears in Deuteronomy 30:19; 31:28; and 32:1. The prophets also make use of those words. All of God's creation witnesses to Israel's sin and disloyalty.

"The LORD your God is a merciful God" challenges our stereotype of the Old Testament God of wrath. Israel will call from exile, and God will hear. God remembers the covenant even when the people of God have sinned and been exiled.

❏ *Deuteronomy 4:32-40.* Our view of Old Testament law as external and mechanical is inadequate. Passages like this reveal the passion and personal commitment in Israel's feeling about the Torah.

The idea of one God underlies much of the Old Testament. However, this passage (verses 35, 39) is one of the few where this idea is clearly stated.

❏ *Deuteronomy 4:44 - 49.* Verse 44 introduces Moses' introduction, which comprises the major part of the Book of Deuteronomy. "Stipulations" appear for the first time as a description of one of the elements in the Torah. The New Revised Standard Version translates the words as "decrees" and *The Revised English Bible* has "precepts."

❏ *Deuteronomy 5:1.* At the beginning of his second speech, Moses recalls the law given at Sinai. Verse 1 represents the whole spirit of Deuteronomy. It goes beyond instruction to exhort the people to obey the law.

❏ *Deuteronomy 5:3.* At first glance, this verse appears to be an error. The Horeb generation had all died during the desert wanderings. However, the point is that the covenant is with Israel in all of her successive generations. Each generation is party to the covenant.

❏ *Deuteronomy 5:6.* Israel's law is based in history. The lawgiver is the Lord who delivered the people from slavery in Egypt.

The law is not a list of things to do to win God's favor. God has already acted to deliver them and has invited them into a covenant relationship. The laws are the specifications of that covenant.

❑ *Deuteronomy 5:7-10.* The first commandment stresses the fact that Israel is to serve only the Lord. The covenant prohibits Israel's worshiping any other god.

The prohibition of images, the subject of the second commandment, is unique in the ancient world. No object in the created world can adequately represent God. That revelation can come only through history and human experience.

❑ *Deuteronomy 5:11-16.* The third commandment (verse 11) warns against using the power of the divine name for empty or unworthy purposes. Invoking the Lord's name or claiming divine support for hurtful, inhumane, or trivial purposes is the concern of the prohibition.

The sabbath commandment (verses 12-15) is the first notable difference of Deuteronomy from the Exodus 20 version of the Decalogue. Exodus bases the rationale for the sabbath on the creation account (Genesis 1:2–2:4). God, after six days of creating, blesses and hallows the seventh day. Deuteronomy, however, appeals to the deliverance from slavery in Egypt as the reason for keeping the sabbath rest and allowing one's servant to do the same.

The fifth commandment addresses persons for whom the extended family is central. Honoring parents insures faithfulness to traditions from generation to generation.

❑ *Deuteronomy 5:17-21.* The last five commandments concentrate on antisocial actions. Human relations are a concern of Israel's covenant with God.

Israelite society defines adultery (verse 18) as extramarital relations involving a married or betrothed woman. Given the patriarchal social structure, the purpose of this law is to protect the man's property and to insure the legitimacy of children, who carry the family name.

The prohibition against false testimony (verse 20) refers to legal proceedings. When cases depend on the testimony of witnesses (two or more), this provision is crucial.

In the tenth commandment, the neighbor's wife is placed ahead of the neighbor's house, which leads the list in Exodus

20:17. Deuteronomy reflects a growing concern for the status of women.

DIMENSION THREE:
WHAT DOES THE BIBLE MEAN TO ME?

Deuteronomy 4:1-8—Adding to the Word

Moses warns Israel not to take away or add to the word of instruction. The covenant people must live with the full covenant law. They must deal with the word of God as it is, not as they wish it to be.

The word of God is to be faced honestly. It is not to be avoided or explained away; explained and clarified, yes, but never discussed for the purpose of escaping its demands.

God's word has always posed problems. On the one hand, it must be interpreted so that it speaks to the culture in which the church finds itself. At the same time, it must retain its distinctive demands of the human experience.

Where do you think the church's message has been molded to fit the culture? What do you see added or taken away from the gospel today? What pressures produce this addiction or subtraction? How can we relate to our culture without losing our distinctiveness as God's people?

Deuteronomy 4:15-24; 5:7-10—Idolatry

Israel's unusual sense of exclusive loyalty and strong prohibition against images sets her apart in the ancient world. Israel believes that no natural objects can adequately represent the Lord. They are all creatures, and God is the Creator.

Israel's sense of God as transcendent creator can help us see our idolatries. If we understand that all meaning comes from God, then we realize that nothing else has ultimate meaning. We often live, however, as if social forces or technological knowledge have purpose and life independent of God's intentions and judgments. This manner of living gives ultimate meaning to things other than God and constitutes idolatry.

What does our society idolize? To what or whom do we give power and control in our lives?

Deuteronomy 5:11—Misusing the Name of the Lord

Most persons apply the third commandment exclusively to the use of profanity. While such use of the divine name is not desirable, the commandment addresses a larger issue. The Israelites understood that they were not to use God's name in the service of empty or wrongful causes.

The church has often claimed the name of God for causes that are not in keeping with divine ends. Some of the medieval crusades are a clear example of this claim. The Inquisition of the sixteenth century used the name of Christ to support the persecution of people whose faith did not meet the approval of the church authorities. In America during World War I, the church and many Christians identified God's will with the United States' objectives.

What individual or church actions can you identify as a vain use of God's name? Where do you think religious leaders or church people are claiming the name of God for positions and movements that are unworthy? divisive? unloving?

Deuteronomy 5:12-15—Observing the Sabbath

Nowhere is the difference between the two accounts of the Ten Commandments more clear than in the fourth commandment. Exodus stresses the sabbath's basis in the Creation story, where God blesses the seventh day. In Deuteronomy, rest for servants is given priority. The root of the observance lies in Israel's historical deliverance from slavery.

What are we to make of these differing accounts? Both agree that the sabbath is important for the covenant people.

The truth is probably found in the combination of reasons for keeping the sabbath. The sabbath reflects God's rest at the culmination of creation. And it also serves as a reminder of the Lord's mighty act of deliverance from bondage. This reminder regularly prods the Israelites to remember how they came into existence. It also calls for humane treatment of one's servants—an awareness of everyone's need for rest. Thus the sabbath for Israel was a part both of their worship of God and their respect for the dignity of human beings.

In the Christian tradition a fundamental shift took place in the early church. Sunday, the day of resurrection, replaced Saturday, the Jewish sabbath, as the day of rest and worship. However, many of the functions of the sabbath remained the same. The church generally has applied Old Testament sabbath instruction to the Christian understanding of Sunday.

What should our use of Sunday take into account? What elements of worship and respect for God are involved? How are this respect and worship related to matters of concern and caring? What opportunities does Sunday give us as Christians?

See, I am setting before you today a blessing and a curse (11:26).

9

Moses Exhorts The People
Deuteronomy 6–11

DIMENSION ONE:
WHAT DOES THE BIBLE SAY?

Answer these questions by reading Deuteronomy 6

1. What is Israel to hear? (6:4)

2. How is Israel to love God? (6:5)

3. What are the Israelites not to forget when they enter Canaan? (6:12)

4. When a son asks about the meaning of the law, what answer is to be given? (6:20-25)

Answer these questions by reading Deuteronomy 7

5. What nations will God clear out before Israel? How is Israel to treat the sacred objects of these peoples? (7:1, 5)

6. Why has the Lord chosen Israel? (7:8)

7. What is the basis of the Israelites' hope when they enter the Promised Land? (7:17-21)

Answer these questions by reading Deuteronomy 8

8. Why does the Lord feed Israel with manna? (8:3)

9. What does Moses warn the Israelites not to do when they settle in the affluence of Canaan? What will happen if they do? (8:11-20)

Answer the questions by reading Deuteronomy 9

10. What arouses the Lord's anger against Israel? (9:11-19)

11. What is the basis of Moses' appeal when he intercedes? (9:26-29)

Answer these questions by reading Deuteronomy 10

12. What is on the second pair of stone tablets? Where does Moses put the tablets? (10:1-5)

13. What kind of God does Israel worship? (10:17-18)

14. What does Moses command Israel to do in response to God? (10:19-20)

Answer these questions by reading Deuteronomy 11

15. What past events is Israel to consider? (11:2-6)

16. Where are the blessing and the curse to be set? What determines which one falls on Israel? (11:26-29)

DIMENSION TWO:
WHAT DOES THE BIBLE MEAN?

❏ *Deuteronomy 6:4-9.* It is not quite clear whether the emphasis in verse 4 is on the uniqueness or the unity of God. If it is the former, then The New Jerusalem Bible translates it correctly, " The LORD is our God, the LORD alone." Israel is to have no other gods.

Another possible meaning is the oneness of God. The Canaanite religion has many local baals. Israel adapts its religion to this setting and installs worship in all the local shrines. This practice opens the people to fertility cult influence and suggests that the Lord can be divided into local deities. In this setting, Deuteronomy may be insisting on the unity of God. The New International Version translation, "Hear, O Israel: the LORD our God, the LORD is one," supports this idea.

The call for love in verse 5 seems strange in a book devoted to law. However, Deuteronomy insists that Israel's willing commitment is essential. The Torah is not imposed as an external set of restrictions. It can function properly only when the people respond to it freely from within.

Jesus quotes Deuteronomy 6:5 as the first or great commandment (Matthew 22:37; Mark 12:30; Luke 10:27).

❏ *Deuteronomy 6:16-19.* The second sermon deals with testing the Lord. The reference to Massah (Exodus 17:1-7) recalls Israel's first complaint after leaving Egypt. There the people demanded proof of God's trustworthiness.

❏ *Deuteronomy 6:20-25.* The third sermon begins with a son's question about the meaning of the divine law. The answer lies in the story of God's deliverance of Israel from Egypt. The law is the basis on which Israel can continue to live in covenant with God.

❑ *Deuteronomy 7:1-5.* The Hittites are remnants of a great kingdom in Asia Minor from 1600 to 1200 B.C. The Amorites, best known in Mesopotamia, are the hill-dwellers in Canaan. The Canaanites are those who live on the plains. Joshua 9:3-7 associates the Hivites with the Gibeonites. The Jebusites are the rulers and inhabitants of Jerusalem prior to David.

The "sacred stones" in verse 5 symbolize the male deity in the fertility cult. "Asherah poles" refer to wooden representations of the female deity.

❑ *Deuteronomy 7:6-16.* "Holy" carries the idea of separateness. Israel as a holy people has been separated from—designated for—a special relationship with God and a special purpose in history. This special relationship is based not on Israel's merit, but on God's love and faithfulness to his promise made to the fathers. Covenant is a gift from God. Obedience is the response that makes blessing possible.

The blessings in verse 13 are things usually attributed to Baal in the Canaanite religion. Fertility is the gift of the Lord, not Baal.

❑ *Deuteronomy 8:1-6.* In verses 2-5, the writer interprets the desert experience as God's test of Israel. The central point is the manna (Exodus 16) on which Israel feeds in the desert. The purpose of the miracle is to teach Israel that the real source of life is not bread but the word of God. As the Israelites anticipate life in the midst of Canaan's agricultural blessings, they must never forget the lessons of the desert.

❑ *Deuteronomy 9:1-5.* The Anakite tradition presents the residents of Canaan as giants (Numbers 13:33; Deuteronomy 1:28). After the Israelites overcome the Anakites, they will be tempted to ascribe the victory to their own righteousness. The real reasons for Israel's success are the Lord's judgment on the wickedness of the previous inhabitants and God's loyalty to the covenant with Israel.

❑ *Deuteronomy 9:7-10:11.* Following the series of short sermons (6:10–9:6), Deuteronomy returns to historical narrative. The theme in the story of the golden calf (Exodus 32) is Israel's rebellious nature. In making a molten calf, the people break the covenant and are subject to judgment. Moses' breaking of the tables is more than an angry response. It signifies that the covenant has already been broken by Israel's sin.

In verses 18-19, Moses successfully intercedes to avert Israel's destruction. His intercessory prayer (9:26-29) appeals to God in three ways: (1) God's past deliverance, (2) God's promise to the patriarchs, and (3) God's divine reputation. If the Lord destroys Israel, the Egyptians would say that God was unable to bring the Israelites to the Promised Land.

Deuteronomy 10:1-5 describes the ark as a container for the two tables of the covenant law. For Deuteronomy, the ark is a box that is important only because it contains the Decalogue. Elsewhere (Numbers 10:35-36; 1 Samuel 4:4), the ark is the throne of God, a symbol of the divine presence.

❏ *Deuteronomy 11:2-9.* Recalling the deliverance events as well as the punishment for Israel's rebelling instructs Israel that God's action is both saving and judging. Verses 8 and 9 also combine love and judgment. They speak of the land as promised to the fathers but make Israel's continued life there subject to the people keeping the law.

❏ *Deuteronomy 11:26-32.* Deuteronomy draws a clear line between life and death, good and evil, blessing and cursing. Blessing follows obedience; cursing follows disobedience.

Verse 29 probably refers to part of the covenant renewal ceremony at Shechem. Mount Gerizim and Mount Ebal are located near Shechem, the former to the south and the latter to the north.

DIMENSION THREE:
WHAT DOES THE BIBLE MEAN TO ME?

Deuteronomy 6:4-9—Love and Law

These verses are some of the best known in the whole Pentateuch. In Judaism they are the core of the *Shema.* Devout Jews recite these three passages of Scripture (Numbers 15:37-41; Deuteronomy 6:4-9; 11:13-21) every day. Jews recite verse 4 in the synagogue service when the Torah scroll is taken from the ark for reading. When Jesus is asked what the first commandment is, he replies by quoting Deuteronomy 6:5, along with Leviticus 19:18.

Verse 4 witnesses to Israel's faith that God is one. Verse 5 gives a second major point. The primary command is to love the Lord with all of one's being. Keeping the law comes from an obedient and committed heart.

Deuteronomy insists that love of God is central to Israel's life in the covenant. Three of the Gospels tell us that Jesus pointed to this passage as the Great Commandment, the ground of the whole law. Is love of God the great commandment for the church in the new covenant? Can it be commanded?

Deuteronomy asks for a responding love. God's love is evident in his acts of deliverance and blessing. Israel's response to deliverance and the gift of the land is to be characterized by love and obedience.

Can the same thing be said of our love of God? In what events do we see God's love for us? How is love for God in the church an expression of gratitude for what God has done?

In Deuteronomy, love is something more than a feeling. It motivates obedience to the law. How does our love express itself? To what service does it move us? In a covenant of grace, what regulations and expectations guide our obedience?

Deuteronomy 6:10-12, 8:7-20
Affluence and Forgetfulness

The writer of Deuteronomy has a keen insight into human nature. When people become affluent, they tend to forget everything but their own efforts and desires. Deuteronomy warns Israel, "When the LORD your God brings you into the land . . . be careful that you do not forget the LORD" (6:10, 12).

Appearances of self-sufficiency are misleading. They lead to disobedience, which cuts off relationship with the source of grace and blessing. Disobedience ignores God's will, obstructing the love to which the covenant calls us.

Deuteronomy challenges our self-understanding and our concept of achievement. Do we credit ourselves with having earned what we have? Is such credit justifiable? Why or why not? What does Deuteronomy's warning say to us?

How do these passages speak to our national life? To what degree is our affluence due to forces and conditions we did not create? What gifts should we acknowledge? How will this acknowledgment affect our use of resources and power?

Deuteronomy 11:26-32—Curse and Blessing

These verses provide the basis of Deuteronomy's theology. The sharp distinction of the two ways and their consequences is an important witness to the fundamental rightness of life.

However, such sharp division presents certain problems. The Old Testament itself raises questions (Job and Psalm 73) about understanding life when it does not fit a neat theological pattern of reward and punishment.

Deuteronomy is certainly aware of the complexity of life and the vagueness of some moral decisions. It reminds us, however, that we must decide which way to go. And our decision makes a difference to the course of life and history.

In our personal lives, questions of right and wrong are often complicated. How can Deuteronomy's concept of the two ways help us in making decisions? How can we keep from becoming self-centered in our moral decisions?

Deuteronomy 6:13, 16; 8:3—Scripture and Temptation

The temptation story in Matthew 4:1-11 (and Luke 4:1-13) uses Deuteronomy. In each of the three temptations, Jesus replies to the devil with a reference to Deuteronomy. Jesus is aware of his tradition and its function in life.

When the devil challenges Jesus, after a long fast, to change stones to bread, Jesus replies with Deuteronomy 8:3. The emphasis is on trust in God's good purposes. Jesus sees the larger issue.

While daring Jesus to throw himself off the pinnacle of the Temple, the devil also cites Scripture to support his case (Psalm 91:11-12). Jesus answers by quoting Deuteronomy 6:16. Here Deuteronomy warns against the kind of faithlessness that forces God's hand. Jesus looks to his heritage and refuses to let his commitment to God depend on God's coming through on demand.

When offered world dominion, Jesus replies by quoting Deuteronomy 6:13. The issue is one of ultimate commitment. Everything is measured by one's total loyalty to God. What does Jesus' use of his scriptural heritage teach us? Is the answer that Deuteronomy 6:13 gives appropriate for us when we are faced with temptation? Why or why not?

Observe the month of Abib and celebrate the Passover of the
LORD your God (16:1).

—— 10 ——
Statutes and Ordinances
Deuteronomy 12–19

DIMENSION ONE:
WHAT DOES THE BIBLE SAY?

Answer these questions by reading Deuteronomy 12

1. Where is Israel to bring offerings, sacrifices, and tithes? (12:5-11)

2. Where may the Israelites slaughter and eat meat? What are they to do with the blood? (12:15-16)

Answer these questions by reading Deuteronomy 13

3. When are the people to ignore the words of a prophet? (13:1-5)

4. What are persons to do when a close relative or friend counsels apostasy? (13:6-10)

5. What will happen to a town that worships other gods? (13:12-18)

Answer these questions by reading Deuteronomy 14

6. What characteristics make an animal acceptable for eating? (14:6) What fish are clean? (14:9)

7. What are the Israelites to do with their tithes if the sanctuary is too far away from them? (14:22-27)

8. Who receives the third-year tithe? (14:28-29)

Answer these questions by reading Deuteronomy 15

9. What is the creditor to cancel in the seventh year? (15:1-2) What attitude are persons to show to the poor? (15:7-11)

10. What is the length of service for a Hebrew slave? (15:12) What if the slave wishes to stay? (15:16-17)

11. What festival are the Israelites to observe in the month of Abib? (16:1) With what is the festival sacrifice to be eaten? (16:2-4)

12. What other festivals are they to keep during the year? (16:10, 13)

13. If a case arises that is too difficult for local decision, what is the person to do? (17:8-13)

14. What four things must a king not do? (17:16-17)

15. What is the king to consult daily throughout his reign? (17:18-20)

Answer these questions by reading Deuteronomy 18

16. What right does a Levite from any town have at the place which the Lord chooses? (18:6-7)

17. How can Israel tell the difference between a prophet who speaks God's word, and one who has a false word? (18:19-22)

Answer these questions by reading Deuteronomy 19

18. Who may use the cities of refuge? (19:1-7)

19. What is the punishment for a false witness? (19:15-20)

DIMENSION TWO:
WHAT DOES THE BIBLE MEAN?

❏ *Deuteronomy 12:1-12.* The words " These are the decrees and laws" introduce the law section of Deuteronomy. The one God (see the *Shema* in 6:4) is to be worshiped in one place. Verse 5 tells us that the Lord will choose the place.

❏ *Deuteronomy 12:13-28.* According to an old custom, slaughter and sacrifices were identical. Now Deuteronomy allows secular slaughter. People can eat meat within their homes as long as they do not eat the blood. And they must still take the required offerings to the sanctuary. Verse 16 and verses 23 and 24 emphasize the biblical view that blood is life, and as such belongs to God.

❑ *Deuteronomy 13:1-18.* In Deuteronomy, turning away from the Lord is a primary sin. The people are to reject the prophet who counsels following other gods, even if he has given a sign and it has come to pass. A sign is usually a predicted event that validates the prophet's word when it happens.

The words at the end of verse 5 occur nine times in Deuteronomy. They express the seriousness with which the writer takes faithlessness.

❑ *Deuteronomy 14:22-29.* Having a central sanctuary presents a problem for the tithe offering. The tithes are portions of the crops, and transporting the tithes to a distant sanctuary is impractical. This passage allows the people to turn their tithe into money. With this money, they can purchase items at the sanctuary to "eat there in the presence of the LORD."

❑ *Deuteronomy 15:1-11.* The Hebrew word for "cancel" in verse 1 comes from the same root as "lie unplowed and unused" in Exodus 23:11. Both passages refer to the seventh year. However, the Exodus passage refers to the land's lying unplowed and unused. In Deuteronomy, we see that an agricultural regulation has been extended to cover another aspect of the economy—loans and debts.

❑ *Deuteronomy 15:12-18.* The Israelites are to release Hebrew slaves after six years. When they go free, the slaves are given means to establish themselves. This practice is based on the memory of the Israelite's similar plight in Egypt. It is interesting that the writer specifically includes women in the law of slaves' release.

❑ *Deuteronomy 16:1-17.* The spring festival, held in the month of Abib (March-April), combines the Feast of Passover and the Feast of Unleavened Bread. Passover was probably a semi-nomadic festival observed at the time of a move to summer pastures. Unleavened Bread was an agricultural festival, marking the beginning of the barley harvest. The Israelites combined the festivals of Passover and Unleavened Bread, and identified both with the Exodus from Egypt.

Deuteronomy states that the Passover animal be sacrificed at the central sanctuary. Elsewhere in the Old Testament, Passover is observed in the home and family setting.

The Feast of Weeks (verses 9-12), which celebrates the last of the grain harvest, is set seven weeks after the first festival. Deuteronomy calls Israel to "rejoice" (verse 11), an emphasis usually associated with ingathering (verse 14). Here, too, the writer includes women in the worshiping community. All the needy persons are intentionally included in the celebration.

In verses 13-15, the Festival of Ingathering (Exodus 23:16; 34:22) is given a different name, *tabernacles*. This name probably refers to the temporary shelters, or "booths," in which farmers stayed during harvest.

❑ *Deuteronomy 17:14-20.* This passage is the only one in the Pentateuch that deals with the office of king. Deuteronomy recognizes the monarchy but puts definite restrictions on it.

The prohibition against multiplying horses is a reference to armed strength and its accompanying pride (Isaiah 2:7-9; Micah 5:10-14). The restriction of the number of wives is to prevent temptation to faithlessness. The third warning refers to multiplication of silver and gold, which leads to unwarranted self-confidence and willfulness. The king is also to avoid feelings of superiority over others.

❑ *Deuteronomy 18:9-22.* Verses 9-14 prohibit all practices that attempt to ascertain the future by magical manipulation. All such activity claims power that belongs only to God.

The writer regards Moses as the model prophet. He speaks for God and serves as a mediator for the covenant people. Verse 18 indicates that this function will continue among the people. God will continue to provide prophets. The people are to heed their word.

How are the hearers to distinguish between true and false prophets? The words of a true prophet will come to pass. But this test is of little help to those who wait between oracle and fulfillment.

❑ *Deuteronomy 19:1-13.* In Israelite society, a person who killed another could flee to the worship center and claim sanctuary at the altar. The cities of refuge arise to offer a more permanent solution to the problem. In Deuteronomy, the cities of refuge are even more crucial, since the altar is no longer nearby due to the centralization of the sanctuary.

❑ *Deuteronomy 19:14-21.* The law that forbids the moving of a landmark, or boundary stone (verse 14), deals with a matter of some concern. It also occurs in the prophets (Isaiah 5:8; Hosea 5:10), in wisdom literature (Job 24:2; Proverbs 22:28; 23:10), and in Deuteronomy's account of covenant renewal at Shechem (Deuteronomy 27:17). By moving the landmarks, the strong could defraud the poor and threaten their livelihood.

The regulation requiring at least two witnesses in criminal matters is important and occurs twice in Deuteronomy (17:6; 19:15.) Verses 16-21 treat the case of the false witness who intends to do harm. The reference in verse 17 to "stand in the presence of the LORD" indicates that the matter has reached the court described in 17:8-13.

DIMENSION THREE:
WHAT DOES THE BIBLE MEAN TO ME?

Deuteronomy 12:1-14—The Unity of God's People

One of the distinctive features of Deuteronomy is its insistence on a single place of worship for Israel. The people are to shun and destroy the local shrines dedicated to the worship of Baal. Only then can Israel's worship be pure.

Deuteronomy's theology grows out of a concern with the negative influences of baalism. Baalism's emphases deny Israel's covenant faith. The central world view of baalism denies the very possibility of a covenant relationship, the basic ground of the life of Israel.

Recognizing the meaning of Deuteronomy's emphasis on unity, do you see any need for this same kind of unity in our day? How will emphasizing unity in worship help to serve the best interests of the church? How can we provide room for experimentation and change?

Deuteronomy 13:1-18—The Seriousness of Disloyalty

Chapter 13 deals with those who tempt the people of God away from the true faith. The punishment in all cases is death. This punishment indicates the seriousness of disloyalty in a time when disloyalty was very tempting.

Deuteronomy is concerned with the result of faithlessness. It tries to prevent it by warning of its dire consequences. Israel must see how terribly wrong such a course of action is. Deuteronomy leaves the message of forgiveness to other Old Testament passages. Its message focuses on the importance of total obedience to the Lord.

Is disloyalty to God as bad as Deuteronomy paints it? Is it really harmful? What is its result? What is the quality of our loyalty? Do we give ourselves wholeheartedly in our faith?

Deuteronomy 15:1-18—God and the Poor

Exodus 23:10-11 and Leviticus 25:1-7 stipulate that the land will lie unplowed and unused every seventh year. This stipulation recognizes that the land belongs to the Lord and is Israel's by gift.

Only Deuteronomy interprets the "sabbatical year" to include cancellation of debts. The idea of the seventh year, which in other rules involves the landholder alone, is expanded so that the cost is distributed more fairly. Verses 12-18 free Israelite slaves after six years' service. The spirit that motivates both practices is the same.

Deuteronomy's humane spirit produces a concept of social order for the covenant people that incorporates economic concerns. The poor and weak in the society are to receive special consideration and attention.

Although we live in a more complex and impersonal economic system, Deuteronomy's message still challenges us in our setting of economic priorities.

Can the social sensitivities of Deuteronomy find expression in our economy? If so, how? How does our faith address the poverty question? In light of our biblical heritage, what is a Christian view of the poor?

STATUTES AND ORDINANCES

Deuteronomy 17:14-20—King and Covenant

This discussion of the king's role shows Israel's view of the monarchy. Among her neighbors, the royal power is absolute and unlimited. In Israel, however, the king rules a covenant people and he, too, is subject to the covenant expectations (2 Samuel 12:1-15; 1 Kings 21:17-22).

Although we do not have a monarchy in our society, the qualities of leadership are an important issue for us. Persons in power are always tempted to be self-centered rather than respecting the needs of all equally.

How would you rephrase the three prohibitions of this passage so that they address political leaders today?

Deuteronomy 13:1-5; 18:15-22
True and False Prophets

One of the pressing issues in ancient Israel is distinguishing between true and false prophets. When prophets differ, how are people to know which one to believe? Deuteronomy says that one can recognize a false prophet when the word he speaks does not come true. This solution raises two difficulties. One is deciding what "takes place" means and the other is waiting for this result to manifest itself.

A second way mentioned here (18:20) and emphasized in Chapter 13 is equally important. No matter what signs a prophet may introduce, he is a false prophet if he advises serving foreign gods. Covenant loyalty is the basic test.

This problem is not confined to ancient times. We get conflicting interpretations of the meaning of events and conditions in our time. As Christians we are called to act on the side of righteousness. But we receive differing claims from persons professing to speak the word of God.

What are our criteria for distinguishing between true and false prophets? How do our prophets differ? How can we find the true word of God? How does the true word relate to covenant loyalty and biblical tradition?

You will be a people holy to the LORD your God, as he promised (26:19).

—— 11 ——
A People Holy to the Lord
Deuteronomy 20–26

DIMENSION ONE:
WHAT DOES THE BIBLE SAY?

Answer these questions by reading Deuteronomy 20

1. Why is Israel not to fear when she goes to war? (20:1)

2. Who is exempt from war service? (20:5-8)

3. If a city refuses Israel's offer of peace, what are the Israelites to do? (20:10-14)

4. Why are the Israelites to completely destroy the nearby cities? (20:15-18)

5. How does the nearest city deal with unsolved murders? (21:1-9)

6. When an Israelite man marries a captive foreign woman, what must he not do? (21:10-14)

7. Where must parents take a rebellious son for judgment? (21:18-19)

Answer these questions by reading Deuteronomy 22

8. What must persons do when they see a neighbor's ox or sheep go astray? (22:1-2)

9. If a man is proved wrong when he makes irresponsible charges against his wife, what is his punishment? (22:13-19)

10. Why is the woman treated differently when suspected adultery takes place in the open country rather than in the city? (22:23-27)

Answer these questions by reading Deuteronomy 23

11. Why are Ammonites and Moabites excluded from the assembly of the Lord? (23:3-4)

12. Why must the Israelites maintain a holy camp? (23:14)

13. What does the Lord detest? (23:18)

Answer these questions by reading Deuteronomy 24

14. Who does the Lord command the Israelites to protect? (24:17)

15. When the Israelites overlook produce in harvesting, for whom shall they leave it? (24:19-22)

Answer these questions by reading Deuteronomy 25

16. How many lashes are allowed as punishment for a crime? Why? (25:1-3)

17. When a man dies without sons, his brother must marry the widow. What happens if he refuses to marry her? (25:5-10)

Answer these questions by reading Deuteronomy 26

18. When the people bring the first fruits to the altar, what do they say God did for them? (26:8-9)

19. What does Israel declare concerning God? (26:17)

20. What does God declare about Israel? (26:18-19)

DIMENSION TWO:
WHAT DOES THE BIBLE MEAN?

❏ *Deuteronomy 20:1-4.* The focus of this chapter is warfare. Israel's "holy war" tradition understands the conquest of the land (and later battles) as the work of the Lord. It is God who brings victory. God requires the Israelites to observe certain stipulations as they fight. Two of these are the ban and priestly participation in the warfare.

❏ *Deuteronomy 20:5-8.* The exemptions from service in verses 5-7 may derive from the general Near Eastern practice. They assume that persons should be allowed to enjoy the blessing of their experiences.

❏ *Deuteronomy 20:10-20.* The latter half of the chapter deals with the conduct of war. They are to offer cities a chance to surrender peacefully. If the city resists, the men are slain, and all other persons and goods become plunder.

The distinction between near and far (verses 15-16) adds another category. Since Deuteronomy regards everything Canaanite as unacceptable to the Lord, verses 16 and 17 stipulate that all nearby cities shall be completely destroyed. Destruction of these cities will prevent the inhabitants from teaching Israel their abominable practices (verse 18). These practices are religious rites related to the worship of Baal or other lesser deities.

❑ *Deuteronomy 21:1-9.* Unsolved killings present a difficult problem. The elders of the nearest city are considered responsible for the killing. They are to kill a heifer in a remote wasteland and wash their hands over it. This act transfers their guilt to the animal. The prayer in verse 8 shows that the effectiveness of the whole procedure lies in God's forgiveness.

❑ *Deuteronomy 22:13-30.* This section contains laws governing sexual relations. Verses 13-21 discuss charges against the virginity of a bride. This law requiring proof of virginity, while it seems unduly demanding of the bride, is far ahead of similar laws in other cultures. This law restricts the man's freedom to make capricious charges.

❑ *Deuteronomy 23:15-25.* Verses 15 and 16 treat the subject of runaway slaves. In contrast to other Near Eastern laws on slavery, this law specifies that runaway slaves shall not be returned. The law probably refers to slaves belonging to foreign masters rather than Israelites slaves.

Verses 17 and 18 treat the practice of cult prostitution, a central feature of fertility religion. The Canaanites believe that this practice, which includes both men and women, stimulates fertility and strengthens the fertility god Baal.

The prohibition of interest on loans to Israelites (verses 19-20) arises out of a strong sense of covenant community. This communal bond is also behind the stipulation about limits on what one may do with a neighbor's crops (verses 24-25).

❑ *Deuteronomy 24:1-9.* Verses 1-4 prohibit the remarriage of a man to a woman he has divorced if she has been married to someone else in the meantime. This same law is reflected in Jeremiah 3:1.

Among the various regulations in verse 5-9, perhaps the most significant, is the prohibition of taking a millstone in pledge (verse 6). The millstone is used every day in the home for grinding grain. Its use as a pledge would seriously affect the life of the needy person.

❑ *Deuteronomy 25:5-10.* Israel attaches a high value to children and family continuity. One expression of this priority is levirate marriage. This law provides that a surviving brother of a man who dies without sons shall marry his dead brother's widow. The first son born to this union carries on the name of the dead brother.

This passage describes how a man who refuses to be a levir may go through a ritual of disgrace. The widow removes her sandal—a sign of renunciation of her estate.

❑ *Deuteronomy 26:1-11.* The words in verses 5-9 that accompany the offering of agricultural products emphasize the historical action of the Lord rather than God's place in nature. Israel's recital, beginning with Jacob (the "wandering Aramean") is remarkable for its focus on historical events—the sojourn and oppression in Egypt, the deliverance, and the divine guidance into the Promised Land. Each generation recites this creed using first person pronouns. In this way, each generation of God's people experiences the mighty acts of God (Exodus and Conquest) firsthand.

❑ *Deuteronomy 26:16-19.* Verse 16 is a closing exhortation for Deuteronomy's law in Chapters 12–26. Verses 17-19 summarize the terms of the fundamental agreement—the covenant between the Lord and Israel.

DIMENSION THREE:
WHAT DOES THE BIBLE MEAN TO ME?

Deuteronomy 20:1-20—God and War

One prominent feature of Deuteronomy is its militant opposition to all elements of Canaanite religion. Moses instructs the people of God to exterminate the Canaanites to prevent being corrupted by them.

This emphasis comes into focus in the laws of warfare found in Chapter 20. The holy war concept asserts that God is the one who does battle with the evil forces of Canaan. Israel is only an instrument in that conflict. The victory of the Lord is certain. Israel plays her part in the struggle by obeying covenant stipulations, including the complete destruction of the Canaanites.

Deuteronomy reminds Israel over and over again that God is at work in history to bring the divine purposes to fulfillment. When we see the sordid and the destructive in our society, can we still believe that God is active? What basis do we have for faith and hope?

Deuteronomy 22:1-4—Hiding From Need

Israelites are to take responsibility for a neighbor's property. When they notice stray animals or lost garments, the law stipulates: "Do not ignore it." Deuteronomy not only commands action; it also prohibits hiding from responsibility.

Much of our wrongdoing consists of "the things we have left undone that we ought to have done." We often avoid ethical and moral responsibility by ignoring situations that call for action. What human needs call for our attention today? In what ways do we conceal ourselves from social responsibility?

Deuteronomy 22:13-21—Advancing Toward Justice

The procedure that places proof of virginity solely on the bride seems unfair to us. We need to realize, however, that this law is a clear advance over the law it replaced. The old law allowed a husband to make charges without restriction. The new law requires the man to prove his charges in a public trial, where he is punished if they prove false.

This law reminds us that we need to question our judicial system when it demands more of some people than of others. What classes or groups of people do not receive equal treatment in our justice system? Where is change needed? What is our Christian responsibility to see that these changes take place?

Deuteronomy 24:10-13, 19-22—Attitude Toward the Poor

These two passages show extraordinary concern for the welfare and dignity of the poor. The first passage, in discussing pledges for loans, stipulates that the creditor has no right to violate the privacy of the debtor's home.

The second passage provides for the feeding of the poor and defenseless. This responsibility was part of custom and law, and was recognized by the whole society (Ruth 2).

What do these laws say to us about our attitude toward the poor? Where does our society violate the dignity of the poor?

Deuteronomy 26:5-10—Tradition and Identity

The liturgy that accompanies the offering of firstfruits (verses 5-9) is striking. Moses asks Israel to remember the historical acts of God while they celebrate a nature festival. All their neighbors worship the gods of nature, but the Israelites witness to the mighty acts of God in history. God's primary relationship with human beings is not through nature, but through their own experiences within history.

The passage also communicates a strong sense of value of tradition. By reciting the past, each new generation comes to know the full meaning of life as God's covenant people in the present.

How does a sense of our past make us more aware of ourselves as the people of God? How can we cultivate the value of tradition in our life and worship?

I set before you today life and prosperity, death and destruction (30:15).

12

Blessings and Curses

Deuteronomy 27–30

DIMENSION ONE:
WHAT DOES THE BIBLE SAY?

Answer these questions by reading Deuteronomy 27

1. What does Moses command Israel to do at Mount Ebal? (27:4-5)

2. Have the Israelites become God's people because they obey the law or must they obey the law because they are God's people? (27:9-10)

3. Which tribes are to stand on Mount Gerizim? Which on Mount Ebal? To do what? (27:11-13)

Answer these questions by reading Deuteronomy 28

4. What will happen to the Israelites if they obey God? (28:1-2)

5. If Israel obeys the Lord, what will be blessed? (28:3-6)

6. If Israel does not obey, what will be cursed? (28:16-19)

7. How will the Lord strike the disobedient people? (28:22)

8. What will happen to Israel's fields, vineyards, and olive trees? (28:38-41)

9. What will the enemy do to Israel? (28:49-52)

Answer these questions by reading Deuteronomy 29

10. What is the purpose of the sworn covenant the Lord makes with Israel? (29:10-13)

11. When the nations ask why the Lord has made the land a desolation, what is the answer? (29:24-26)

Answer these questions by reading Deuteronomy 30

12. If Israel has a change of heart and returns to the Lord while in exile, what will the Lord do for the people? (30:1-3)

13. What will happen when the Lord circumcises the heart of the people? (30:6)

14. What two ways does Moses set before the people? (30:19-20)

DIMENSION TWO: WHAT DOES THE BIBLE MEAN?

❏ *Deuteronomy 27:1-8.* Moses' concern in this passage is to begin Israel's worship in a proper manner as soon as the people arrive in the Promised Land. Worship is to begin on the very day Israel crosses the Jordan.

The law is to be inscribed on plastered stones (verse 2). The Old Testament frequently mentions memorial stones that serve as reminders of the covenant. But this is the only time that such stones have something written on them.

The instruction concerning the altar refers to "fieldstones" and prohibits the use of a metal tool. Exodus 20:24-25 states that no tool shall be used on an altar stone, lest the altar be profaned.

❑ *Deuteronomy 27:11-13.* These verses are probably a fragment of a covenant renewal ceremony at Shechem (Joshua 24). The choice between the mountains as to which represents blessings and which represents curses is probably based on their location. Facing east—the common reference point in the ancient world—Ebal is to the left, the side of misfortune. Gerizim, to the right, is on the side usually associated with good fortune.

The two groups are stationed on opposite sides. The passage reflects a liturgy of blessing and curse. On the Ebal side are Reuben and Naphtali, Leah's oldest and youngest sons, and the four so-called concubine tribes. The Gerizim group includes Leah's other four sons and Rachel's two sons.

❑ *Deuteronomy 27:14-26.* This section is a list of twelve curses, representing the twelve tribes. This list differs from most curse lists, since it does not specify the consequences of violating the prohibitions.

The first curse in the series (verse 15) is the only one that deals directly with worship. The last curse (verse 26) is general in nature and appears to be a summary. In between are ten curses of similar nature. The first four (verses 16-19) govern conduct that violates someone's rights or denies help to the needy. The next four (verses 20-23) involve forbidden sexual relations. The last two (verses 24-25) deal with murder and related bribery.

The people say "Amen!" in response to each curse. The Hebrew word *amen* indicates firmness or surety. In the covenant litany, the word implies assent and commitment.

❑ *Deuteronomy 28:3-6, 16-19.* The language and form of these two sections correspond exactly. Perhaps these blessings and curses are a part of the liturgy from the covenant ceremony such as the one described in 27:11-13. The terms "in the city" and "in the country" (verse 3) probably express totality, meaning "everywhere." The same is true of "when you come in" and "when you go out" (verse 6), meaning "all that you do." The reference to the basket and kneading-trough is strikingly simple and mundane. It applies to fruit gathered in baskets, and grain processed in the kneading-trough.

❏ *Deuteronomy 28:15- 46.* The curse section of Chapter 28 is more extensive than the passage devoted to blessings. Some curses correspond to the blessings in verses 7-14 (for example, verse 23 with verse 12; verse 25 with verse 7) but no regular pattern exists. The curses range from physical affliction (verses 22, 27-35) to frustration of expectations (verses 30-31, 38-42), and oppression by foreign nations (verses 25, 33, 36-37).

❏ *Deuteronomy 28:58-68.* " The Lord will scatter you" (verse 64) expresses one of the main themes in this section. Disobedience has brought the curse of exile from the beloved land.

The absence of rest and the constant wandering (verse 65) are reminiscent of the desert experience. A similar reversal of God's acts of deliverance is found in verse 68, which states "the LORD will send you back in ships to Egypt." This threat undoes all that is central to Israel's faith.

❏ *Deuteronomy 29:1-9.* Verse 1 marks a major transition in the Book of Deuteronomy. The next verse, Deuteronomy 29:2, begins Moses' third address. Like the first two, this third address (29:2–30:20) stresses faithful obedience. But now Moses demands obedience to a covenant law that is complete and lies before the people.

❏ *Deuteronomy 29:10-15.* All of Israel—the leaders, ordinary men and women, children, "aliens living in your camps who chop your wood and carry your water"—stands before God to enter into the covenant. The covenant establishes all Israel as God's people and the Lord as their God.

Verses 14 and 15 provide for future generations to become members of the covenant. The covenant is with all Israel, present and future.

❏ *Deuteronomy 30:15-20.* Moses concludes the final address with a challenge to the people. He has described the covenant. He has exhorted Israel to be loyal and obedient. Finally, all that remains is the categorical imperative. Two ways are open. They are life and death. Moses says, "Choose life." Verse 20 explains this choice as requiring Israel to "love the LORD your God, listen to his voice, and hold fast to him."

BLESSINGS AND CURSES   **99**

DIMENSION THREE:
WHAT DOES THE BIBLE MEAN TO ME?

Deuteronomy 27:9-10—Grace and Ethics

The most important truth of these verses is the underlying assumption about the relationship between covenant and obedience. Israel's covenant existed prior to any obedience on Israel's part. The covenant is a gift of God, who initiates the relationship not on the basis of goodness but on the basis of love (Deuteronomy 7:7-11.)

On the other hand, Deuteronomy asserts that obedience to the covenant is a primary expectation in the life of Israel. Most of Deuteronomy emphasizes obedience, specifying a wide range of statutes and ordinances to be observed.

Although Christianity does not give the central place to the Torah that Judaism does, we have the same problem with integrating salvation and ethical responsibility. We often divide ourselves into two camps—one emphasizing salvation and piety, the other stressing social action. Too many of us agree to this separation.

Why do we have problems putting grace and social action together? Do our ethics reflect what we believe about God? How so? Can we be satisfied with a view of salvation that involves only God and the individual Christian? How does our relationship with God in Christ affect our relationship with all our brothers and sisters?

Deuteronomy 28:1-6, 15-19—Blessing and Curse

These limited selections from a long chapter that deals with blessings and curses set before us one of the key concepts of Deuteronomy. God judges oppression and faithlessness and gives life to those who remain loyal and obedient to the divine will. Seemingly, the righteous prosper and the wicked suffer.

Deuteronomy applies this idea of divine retribution primarily to the nation. All of Israel prospers when obedient, and all of Israel suffers when disobedient. This approach is a significant witness to the moral nature of God's rule over history. In later times, when persons begin to apply retribution theology to individual experience, it raises difficult problems. These problems arise from real life where often the righteous suffer and the wicked prosper. Job, Ecclesiastes, and several of the psalms challenge the retribution concept seriously.

How often do you operate out of the idea of blessings and curses? What other factors do you consider when dealing with individual experience? How do you relate retribution to Christian suffering? Where and how does the cross fit into your understanding of suffering?

Deuteronomy 29:2-4—Eyes That Do Not See

Here Deuteronomy recounts the struggle with Pharaoh and the deliverance from Egypt. The trials, the signs, the wonders—these are all done in Israel's presence. But Israel missed the point! Verse 4 phrases it, " The LORD has not given you a mind that understands." God's mighty acts have taken place within Israel's experience, but the people have not understood the meaning of covenant or the God who is its source. They continue to misread events, going after other gods and ignoring their covenant responsibilities.

A historical event has two dimensions: the physical happening and its interpretation. The meaning we give to events is a crucial aspect of human experience. In our understanding of history and present experience, we often fail to see life's deepest meanings. This failure keeps us from life's fullest possibilities.

Where in current events do we give different interpretations to the same situation or happening? How can we tell which interpretation is valid? What is a Christian reading of events in our time?

Deuteronomy 30:15-20—Choose Life!

Moses' final "sermon" to Israel challenges Israel to choose a course. Two ways exist. One leads to life, one to death. Deuteronomy says, "Choose life."

Knowing the complexities of life, can we believe with Deuteronomy that we have only two courses of action open to us? Are certain courses of action deadly in our world? How does the idea of two ways apply to national policy? What implication does it have for individual choices and lifestyle? What has Deuteronomy contributed to your understanding of the way to life?

Since then, no prophet has risen in Israel like Moses
(34:10).

13
Epilogue
Deuteronomy 31–34

DIMENSION ONE:
WHAT DOES THE BIBLE SAY?

Answer these questions by reading Deuteronomy 31

1. How does Moses encourage Israel when he says he will not be going to Canaan? (31:3-7)

2. What does Moses instruct the priests and elders to do with the law? (31:10-11)

3. Where does the Lord tell Joshua to go? (31:23)

4. Where does Moses tell the Levites to put the Book of the Law? (31:24-26)

5. What does Moses expect to happen after his death? (31:27-29)

Answer these questions by reading Deuteronomy 32

6. In Moses' song, who does he say is the Lord's portion and allotted inheritance? (32:9)

7. What response does Moses say that Israel made to God? (32:15-18)

8. What prevents God from bringing punishment on Israel? (32:26-27)

9. What will the Lord do for Israel? (32:36)

10. Where does the Lord tell Moses to go? What will Moses do there? (32:48-50)

Answer these questions by reading Deuteronomy 33

11. What is Deuteronomy 33? (33:1)

12. What persons are mentioned in the poem? (33:6, 7, 8, 12, 13, 18, 20, 22, 23, 24)

13. What responsibilities does Moses give to Levi? (33:10)

Answer these questions by reading Deuteronomy 34

14. What does the Lord show Moses from the mountain top? (34:1-4)

15. Where is Moses buried? (34:5-6)

16. How old is Moses when he dies? How long does Israel mourn for him? (34:7-8)

17. What marks Moses as a unique prophet? (34:10-12)

DIMENSION TWO:
WHAT DOES THE BIBLE MEAN?

The last four chapters of Deuteronomy pick up the story of the Israelites where the Book of Numbers ended. Moses has finished giving Israel the law. He has declared the blessings and curses of the covenant, and the admonitions to be faithful to God and obedient to the covenant are completed in Chapter 30. The final four chapters include the installation of

Joshua as Moses' successor; two extended poems, one about God's relationship with Israel and the other, Moses' final blessing; and the account of Moses' death.

❏ *Deuteronomy 31:9-13.* This passage refers to a law that Moses wrote and entrusted to the Levites. This law is the main body of Deuteronomy (Chapters 5–26). The law is to be read every seven years (the year of release mentioned in Chapter 15) at the fall festival. This festival was probably related to the annual covenant renewal ceremony celebrated at Shechem in the early days of Israel's life in Canaan.

❏ *Deuteronomy 31:24-29.* Moses commands the Levites to deposit his writing of the law next to the ark of the covenant so it will be remembered. The Ten Commandments are already in the ark, and this law (Deuteronomy) is placed alongside because it is equally important.

❏ *Deuteronomy 32:1-6.* The song of Moses begins with a call for heaven and earth to witness the charges that Moses brings against Israel. The song is built on the form of a covenant lawsuit. Israel has violated the covenant, and God is bringing charges against the people.

The word *Rock* in verse 4 refers to God. The same word occurs five other times in the course of the poem (verses 15, 18, 30, 31, 37). The word *Rock*, when used as a title for God, emphasizes the characteristics of constancy and strength.

Verse 6 speaks of God "who made you and formed you." This "you" refers to the creation of Israel as a people rather than to individual creation.

❏ *Deuteronomy 32:15-18. Jeshurun* (verse 15) is a poetic name for Israel. The origin and meaning of this word are unknown. Jeshurun may bear some relationship to *yashar,* the Hebrew word for "upright."

Going a step beyond Creator and Maker, verse 18 speaks of God using the figure of Parent. " The Rock, who fathered you" and "the God who gave you birth" portray the relation of God to Israel as parent to child.

❏ *Deuteronomy 32:26-27.* In the usual course of events, the apostasy and rebellion that Israel shows would bring the judgment of God on the covenant partner. But verses 26-27 describe a surprising turn in the Lord's thought. If God were to

NUMBERS AND DEUTERONOMY

punish Israel, her enemies would misinterpret God's action. They would suppose they had brought about Israel's downfall, not realizing that God was using them to punish the chosen people. Their lack of understanding changes the fortune of Israel.

❑ *Deuteronomy 32:34- 43.* After God's change of heart, God directs his action not to punishment, but rather to vindication of Israel. This surprising turn of events enables the Israelites to see beyond judgment to restoration and continuation of the covenant.

❑ *Deuteronomy 32:48-52.* This account gives one reason why Moses was not allowed to enter Canaan. Verse 51 says that God is punishing Moses for a sin he committed at Meribah Kadesh (Numbers 20:1-13; 27:14). Elsewhere in Deuteronomy, Moses' death before entering Canaan is attributed to the sins of the people (Deuteronomy 1:37; 3:26.)

❑ *Deuteronomy 33:1-29.* Just as a father blesses his children before his death (see Jacob's blessing in Genesis 49), Moses blesses the Israelites, with whom he has labored for over forty years.

The introduction (verses 2-5) and conclusion (verses 26-29) of the blessing taken together are a hymn of praise, recounting the times when God has shown love toward Israel. The main part of the poem includes ten separate segments. Some parts are wishes, while others are prayers, statements, or maxims. Only two are blessings (verses 13-17, 20-21).

Moses blesses the twelve tribes. Levi, who is not in the Numbers census lists, is included here. Simeon is absent. The blessing includes both of Joseph's sons, Ephraim and Manasseh. The order of the tribes is related to geographical location. The blessing moves from south (Reuben, Judah, Levi) to central (Benjamin, Ephraim, Manasseh) to north (Zebulun, Issachar, Gad, Dan, Naphtali, Asher).

❑ *Deuteronomy 34:1-6.* In this final narrative of the Pentateuch, Moses ascends Mount Nebo and looks across to the Promised Land. The Lord shows him the full extent of the territory Israel is to possess. This viewing is Moses' final act on behalf of Israel.

DIMENSION THREE:
WHAT DOES THE BIBLE MEAN TO ME?

Deuteronomy 31:9-13—The Meaning of Tradition

Everything Moses does here is intended to keep the covenant law alive in the life of Israel. He specifies that the law
receive specific attention on a yearly basis as part of Israel's
religious life and worship. This covenant renewal ceremony is
probably an annual event, perhaps a part of the fall festival.
To this requirement, Moses adds a special seventh-year requirement, the reading of Deuteronomy's covenant law. This
law is to be read in the presence of the whole Israelite congre-
gation. The people are to pay particular attention to children
and their awareness of the religious heritage and tradition.
The purpose of these specifications is to enable people to
"learn to fear the LORD your God" and to live in obedience to
the covenant.

Today we are often impatient with tradition and repetition.
We tend to avoid customs or requirements that require us to
do something on a regular basis. As a result we lose much of
the meaning of our individual past, as well as our heritage.

How can we keep our personal history and its claim on us
alive in succeeding generations? What events in our history do
we need to remind ourselves about from time to time? Many
church traditions include a service of covenant renewal at the
beginning of each year. In light of our study, what is the value
of this service?

Deuteronomy 32:15-18—Affluence and Waywardness

Israel, "the apple of his eye" (verse 10), has received care,
protection, and sustenance from God's hand. The numerous
gifts of the land, listed in verse 14, are evidence of God's care.
And now all this affluence has produced willfulness and rebellion.

One of Deuteronomy's main concerns is the fate of the
Israelites when they settle in Canaan. Over and over again, like
a refrain, Moses warns the people not to forget God when they

settle amidst the blessings of the land. The irony of forgetting God is that God is the one who has given the blessings. Apostasy, or disloyalty, is not only insensitivity to the relationship with God. For Deuteronomy this ungrateful willfulness breaks the covenant and is certain to bring God's judgment.

A similar issue confronts us today. Human nature misinterprets blessing and affluence as callously today as it did in ancient times. Prosperity seems to breed insensitivity toward our responsibility to others and to God.

In what situations today do comfort and wealth produce disdain for God and callousness toward the needs of others? Where does this waywardness happen among nations? Where does such forgetfulness appear in our personal lives? Do affluent Americans need Deuteronomy's warning?

At times in its history, the church has been prosperous and wealthy. During these times, it has tended to identify itself with the interests of the wealthy and has forgotten its mission to the poor and needy. When does the church today follow Israel in her apostasy? In our program and building decisions, have we forgotten what God calls us to be? What positive steps can we take to counteract our insensitivity to the church's mission?

Deuteronomy 32:45-47—Trifle or Word of Life?

In his last exhortation Moses urges the Israelites to take the covenant words to heart, to obey them, and to pass them on to their children. In verse 47, he says, " They are not just idle words for you—they are your life." The law of the Lord's covenant is the word of God. The law is life-giving, but those to whom it is given may regard it as a trifle and miss its dynamic vitality. The Hebrew words that the NIV translates as "idle words" literally mean "empty words."

The Old Testament speaks of the word of the Lord as a dynamic, creative force in life. Genesis 1 says that God created by word. When the prophets speak, they declare the active word of God. Isaiah 55:11 portrays the word as the effective agent of divine purpose. And the New Testament, in John 1, speaks of the " Word made flesh."

Deuteronomy reminds us that God's dynamic word may be regarded as empty in meaning and thus ignored. The Bible insists that life comes through this word. The decision to take the word seriously is a matter of life and death.

In what form does the word of life come to us as Christians? In what ways do we treat it as an "empty word"? How do we take God's word seriously?

Deuteronomy 34—Giants Die; Life Goes On

Most persons agree that Moses was a religious giant in the history of the human race. Deuteronomy 34:10-12 describes Moses as unique in his direct contact with God and in his accomplishment as God's agent in delivering Israel from Pharaoh. In other places in the Pentateuch, we read about his humility, his willingness to give himself for his people, and his outstanding leadership.

These characteristics are true measure of his greatness. And the existence of Israel is a monument to his accomplishments. Deuteronomy 34:1-2 reminds us, however, that death comes to everyone. Heroes die, but life and history go on.

Verse 8 says that the people mourned for a month after Moses' death. Verse 9 tells us about Joshua, Moses' successor. Joshua is not a duplicate of Moses and, as verses 10-12 testify, he does not "fill Moses' shoes." But Joshua is full of the spirit of wisdom. His leadership enables Israel to move on in obedience to the Lord's commandments. The continuity of history comes from the activity and purposes of God.

What crises have resulted from the deaths of great leaders? How does history move on? How do God's purpose and action provide continuity for our life and history?